THE WAR LETTERS
OF AN ENGLISH BURGHER

THE WAR LETTERS
OF AN ENGLISH BURGHER

REGGIE MOSTYN CLEAVER
AND MARGUERITE DE FENTON

Original Preface by Manfred Nathan
Introduction by Stephen Gray

PROTEA BOOK HOUSE
PRETORIA
2000

THE WAR LETTERS OF AN ENGLISH BURGHER
Reggie Mostyn Cleaver and Marguerite de Fenton

Originally published as *A Young South African* by W. E. Hortor, 1913
Reprinted by the State Library, 1974

Second edition, 2000, published by:

Protea Book House
PO Box 35110, Menlo Park, 0102
protea@intekom.co.za

with an introduction © by Stephen Gray, 2000

Typography & design by ANTWORKS Layout & Design
Cover design by HOND BK
Reproduction by Dusk Dimensions
Printed and bound by Interpak Books, Pietermaritzburg

ISBN 1-919825-27-4

© All rights reserved.
** No part of this book may be reproduced in any form, without prior permission in writing from the publisher.

CONTENTS

Introduction 1

Select Bibliography 41

Original Preface vii

The War Letters
I. War Clouds 1
II. At the Front—In Cronje's Laager 34
III. The Prieska Expedition (1900) 49
IV. On to Kenhardt and back to the Rand 81
V. The Last Effort 100
VI. Off to Ceylon 116
VII. The Last Commando 187

Index 201

INTRODUCTION

HE original edition of this book was superbly printed in London, by Charles Whittingham and Co. of Tooks Court, off Chancery Lane near Fleet Street, at the well-known Chiswick Press. This adjoined the office of *The New Age*, the progressive weekly journal which had long supported the Pro-Boer movement in Britain and now through its South African literary editor, Beatrice Hastings, maintained an interest in the younger figures working for a new order of peace and justice in the Union of South Africa. The date of publication was 1913, which explains the lavish style that makes it the kind of collector's item we shall seldom see again.

The covers were of green boards, the spine of quarter Japanese vellum with gilt lettering. The groups of 16 pages of handmade paper, watermarked with a raging lion, were deckle

Original frontipiece of A Young South African

Introduction 3

edged and uncut, so that surviving copies often show the results of unskilled paperknifing. Tipped in opposite the title page, and protected with a sheet of tissue-paper, was the nearly full-length photogravure photograph of the main subject – with his owlish glasses, shaven head and wild moustache, ceremonially dressed to receive his qualifications at the Law Courts near Chancery Lane, with his inky signature as if freshly written beneath it. In reference works describing his life, this is the portrait commonly reproduced.

The title page itself was printed in two colours (black, with iron-red for the title and for the publisher). It read as follows:

A Young South African

A MEMOIR OF
FERRAR REGINALD MOSTYN CLEAVER
ADVOCATE AND VELDCORNET

EDITED BY
HIS MOTHER

The page included a triangular vignette, typical of the ornamental chapter incipits and decorative panels that gave the work a classically controlled, but Art Nouveau look. The text was set in hot lead in a typeface which, with its interesting antique ligature between each 'c' combined with 't', is now difficult to identify.

Proof-reading must also have been done in London, strictly following F. Howard Collins' *Authors' and Printers' Dictionary* of 1905, as spellings which were no longer approved of within modernising, Afrikaans-speaking South Africa ('veldt', 'kopje') adhered to British norms. Nor were other 'foreign' spellings ('Havannah', 'Dyatalawa' for 'Diyatalawa') always correct. This text is reproduced here in facsimile – that is, with errors and all, as it was finalised at the printers – so that the reader may savour its typographical elegance.

There can be little doubt that the original *A Young South African* was what is called a vanity publication, the production costs paid for by the grieving mother in question. It was intended by her to be distributed to the family and friends of her late son, and to other well-wishers who felt that the story of all the English-speaking Boer collaborators – staunch republicans and the 'new' South Africans of

Introduction

that fin de siècle – was being overlooked and forgotten. Indeed, the original dedication was "to the many friends who still hold my son in affectionate remembrance". She meant the book as a memorial to, or a souvenir of, that generation. Over time its uniqueness and poignancy have turned it into far more.

The publisher she used – W. E. Hortor and Co., Ltd., of Johannesburg – must have been merely the distributor, arranged through a long-standing colleague in law like Manfred Nathan (1875–1945), for even then Hortor's was noted as a legal publisher.

From Nathan's preface to the original edition, reproduced here, the reader still has a lively and informative lead into the work. His was not the sole attempt to present the Cleaver story to the public, however. In 1974 the State Library (now the Pretoria branch of the National Library) arranged for a reprint, using as a new preface an article by Roy Macnab which had appeared in 1970 to mark the centenary of F. R. M. Cleaver's birth. This now served to introduce the work afresh to a new generation.

With the centenary of the Anglo-Boer War in which Cleaver perished in such a ghastly manner (on 18 November, 1900, aged 29) upon us, the present reprint is timely once again.

But there is another reason to commemorate Cleaver's work. Like Deneys Reitz of *Commando* (1929), he was not only uniquely situated, but a fine and interesting writer. And clearly he wrote for an audience beyond his immediate family circle, with all the training he could summon in English rhetoric to make him a winning penman. It is a pleasure to (re)encounter this brilliant youth, who was known to his intimates as 'Reg', or sometimes just as 'Dick' – but for whom, he being gangly and well over six foot, 'Reggie' was the endearing nickname those who loved him preferred to use.

However, this Reggie Cleaver was not the only writer in the family. By no means to be forgotten is that very dedicated mother of his, who pulled the whole project together, collecting Reggie's letters from many sources, investigating all the finicky details of place and date, painstakingly cutting and pasting up her album, while outlining her own part in the story. She chose to be self-effacing, not even attaching her own name to the work beyond her married initials (M. M. C.). But, in fact, as the reader will

Introduction

readily notice, a sizeable and vital portion of the book is written by her in the form of connective commentary. Nowadays we would judge that she merits the status of co-author, at least. She had in any case established a modest name of her own as an author – she was Marguerite de Fenton, who died only three years later (in 1916). Long before, she had produced the earliest collection of South African short stories ever to find a local publisher. (This was *Tales Written in Ladybrand*, printed in the office of the O. F. S. Newspaper Co. in Bloemfontein by C. Borckenhagen in 1885, which beat Mrs Mary Ann Carey-Hobson's publication to it by a year.)

Nor was she the sole published author in the immediate family. Uncle Reginald Fenton, the one addressed in young Reggie's letter on p. 162 and elsewhere – not that the pining nephew could have known this – was also to pen a rackety memoir of his South African life, inspired by the story of his gutsy relation. To embellish the title page of this, he linked Reggie in a figure of eight double cameo with his friend, the stalwart old Vice-President and Commandant General, Piet Joubert (1831–1900), as the first South Africans. Today

Introduction

Fenton's dedication to his book is of interest: it is to all those who take their stand upon the unifying fact that "Africa is our Mother Country, not Europe".

Reginald Fenton's work was privately published as well – in 1905, by the so-called 'Pretoria Publishing Co.' in Girard, Kansas, to which he must by then have moved from golden California. The title was the memorable and buoyant *Peculiar People in a Pleasant Land: A South African Narrative* – another collector's item, and one which gives much glee to Africana librarians; in 1908 copies were distributed for sale by R. L. Esson in Johannesburg, so it is not unknown here. Set mostly in the 1860s, it recounts how he, Reginald Fenton, the poverty-stricken greenhorn from the English Midlands, with his tenderfoot best mate, the moody and cursed Mostyn Cleaver, sail away on an Aberdeen windjammer to seek their fortunes in Natal Colony. They become itinerant traders in upcountry truck (picks, beads, brass wire, baftas and punjums), investors in the wool business and freebooters in the various Basotho Wars. Settled in the so-called Conquered Territory of the eastern Orange

Introduction 9

Free State, they come to prosper, as stoor as any of their fellow Boers. Although part of the clan remained attached to their language (English) and to their heritage (the best of British customs and education), as Marguerite's own writing makes clear, Uncle Reginald came so to disagree with his relative's political loyalty to the Union Jack that, like her son Reggie, he threw in his lot with the republican cause. Reading between the lines of his work, one realises that he had so dreaded the militarised Empire taking over his rural Afrikaner paradise, his new Motherland under the Southern Cross, that he had decamped and emigrated to the United States. From there he issued his merry corrective about how the gorgeous country of his middle years could no longer be fit for the *real* English-speakers. Young Reggie, we see, in the event of a British victory at the end of the war, and to avoid being tried for any treachery, was planning to defect and join him, to start over again in the home of the brave.

The reader will gather the salient points of Reggie's biography and of the lives around him piecemeal from Nathan's preface, from his own accounts and from his mother's usefully supportive editorialising. None the less, some details which those close to him considered too personal and thus suppressed need to be retrieved and filled in.

Reggie Cleaver was born on 12 December, 1870, on a farm in the Conquered Territory called Zuringkrans. This is usually given as in the Bethlehem District of the Free State. At the Bethlehem Museum recently I discovered that the district then stretched from Witzieshoek all the way to Kroonstad, and that when after the last Basotho War in 1872 President Brand delimited its extent, he used the edge of Zuringkrans as part of its western boundary and specifically excluded it. Today the farm is four to the west of the hamlet of Paul Roux, on the north edge of the N5 to Senekal (in his letters Reggie often refers to their friends in the old Senekal area). Names of the surrounding farms spell out the story of that border corridor: Alton, Dorset, Schleswig-Holstein, Riga, Mons, Loos, Labrador, Concordia.

The outstanding local geographical feature is the bulky tabletop Zuringkop, which gives vantage over the plains of khaki savannah and grassland and over the Witteberg, and from which two perennial springs flow down to the lesser Zuringkrans. Clambering up that, one gets an immense panorama of rank upon rank of the Drakensberg or Maluti Mountains. The farmstead was built among sorrels in the shelter of the krans, with to this day dassies basking, rooikatte. By the time they intersect the farm property, the springs have become the Debeerspruit, at which the Cleaver establishment would offer a safe crossing, a change of draft animals and later a hostelry; accordingly they grew forage for winter and bred horses.

The imposing farmhouse of dressed sandstone, with its sweeping veranda and two-foot thick walls built to withstand snowy winters, dates to 1886, by which time the Cleavers may well have moved on. But, at any rate, the present owner cordially showed me the foundations of his barn and outhouses, where Mrs Cleaver held what Nathan called her elementary 'dame-school'. An early pupil to be thwacked into controlling his chalk and reciting his tables was the future Chief Justice Jaap de Villiers, the near age-mate of Reggie, who likewise attended his first classes down on the farm. At the bottom of the old walled-off vegetable patch, an immense willow surrounded by syringas – which Reggie must have been told had been brought by the missionaries all the way from India to shelter their dead.

At the Bethlehem Museum, as in many other repositories in the Free State, are kept as treasured mementoes the objects which remind one of the end of the affair for so many strapping burghers from hereabouts. In display cabinets are decorative picture frames, ivory brooches, wire puzzles, pairs of serviette rings, paper knives and miniature musical instruments made from simple materials to hand and without sophisticated tools. These are beguiling objects to touch the hearts of their captors and to swap for salt, for tobacco. Most of the items are from Diyatalawa Camp in Ceylon, to which local prisoners of war, rounded up mostly with Cronje at Paardeberg, or later with Prinsloo, were despatched.

According to Reginald Fenton, the dry climate at Zuringkrans so suited his fellow immigrant partner, the cadaverous Cleaver Senior, that he not only recovered from that curse of tuberculosis, but turned into the bronzed, bearded athlete Joseph Cleaver. He

Introduction

soon married Marguerite (who inevitably became rendered as Margaretha or just Magriet). Together they produced five children – three boys including the youngest, Reggie, together with his two sisters Anne (1866–1922) and Letitia (or Let, see p. 78), planned as the recipients of the lengthy account begun on p. 128 and referred to elsewhere. The oldest member of the immediate family was Marguerite's feisty mother, who lived with her through thick and thin (until she died in 1908). About her, very specific details are known: she was born in Lincolnshire, her father the Anglican rector of Waltham at Great Grimsby; she gave her profession as teacher, was married and widowed soon. Interestingly enough, she kept her maiden name, the very British-sounding Myfanwy Mary Fenton, and travelled to South Africa as a single parent where it was her daughter, Marguerite France, who persuaded her to Frenchify themselves as 'de Fenton'. She too remained loyal to the British royal family, judging from the fact that her most prized possession, which she left to her admirable offspring as her sole support in her last illness (although she had other descendants), was a gold brooch awarded her by Queen Alexandra.

Marguerite de Fenton (right) with her daughter Anne Fenton Cleaver (left) with young Reggie between them

Introduction 15

The memoir Marguerite wrote of her life with Joseph, who in turn took to calling himself Mostyn Cleaver as if the surname were double-barrelled, is regrettably untraceable. But what is known is that, by the onset of the Second Anglo-Boer War, she had lost not only her husband, but also two of their three boys. When she refers to Reggie on p.122 as her only and last son, imploring him to come back safe and sound, we may fully understand the desperate condition in which force of circumstances had placed the Yeoville cottage of Cleaver women.

From the farm Reggie was sent to Saint Andrew's and to Grey College in Bloemfontein, where he fell under the Dutch-born educationalist, Dr Johannes Brill. He had been the rector of the latter since 1873, when it had only 40 pupils, but he built it up to over 200 pupils by the end of the century, half of them boarders. Although he wrote to Mrs Cleaver in English (see p. 188), Brill was an early champion of the use of Afrikaans (as opposed to High Dutch) as an official and literary language. Undoubtedly there Reggie learned to flourish as a budding patriot, adept in both his language heritages without having to face any question of being forced to choose between them. There he was prepared up to the matric level of the University of the Cape of Good Hope. Either from his farm days, or from school, dates his friendship with the family of the old Ignatius Ferreira (who lived in the Senekal District, led the Ladybrand and other commandos at the Battle of Magersfontein and succeeded General C. R. de Wet as Chief Commandant, before being accidentally shot at Paardeberg). The old patriarch had seven sons, including Cornelis (correct spelling – 1877–1932) who served as his campaign secretary (see his letter to Marguerite on p. 192), and who together with two other sons was taken prisoner at the Brandwater Basin. Jan Brink, the great chronicler of the Ceylon diaspora, also served in the Ladysmith Commando and was adjutant to General Crowther. The letters contain several references to other associates of Reggie. Worth recalling is that, when the small landlocked republic centred on flowering Bloemfontein was at last invaded early in 1900 by his own mother's pillaging people, the finest of the British left-wing correspondents to accompany them, the socialist Henry Nevinson, was

Introduction

outraged: he considered that the now ruined Orange River Colony had once been one of the best governed and most orderly countries of the nineteenth-century world.

While still in his teens, however, lanky Reggie won a bursary from the Free State government to study law at the heart of the Imperial metropolis. He completed his LL. B. at the Middle Temple and was admitted to the bar in June, 1892. Details of his early career there are rather legendary, but supposedly he was involved in the sensational trial of the Tower Hill Anarchists and with various murderers, saboteurs and so on. Presumably he could have settled into a modest career within the decadent lifestyle of the globe's largest and most affluent capital. At his fingertips he had the new Aesthetic Movement in the arts, as so much of his style betrays, he knew his Alfred Lord Tennyson (see p. 24), toured suitable cultural locations on the Continent and of course learnt all the private routines of public legal and government matters. But like some powerful Afrikaner figures before him – President F. W. Reitz himself, who treated Reggie like an adopted son, J. C. Smuts, Eugène N. Marais – he

Portrait of the young advocate, taken in Johannesburg

obviously felt the tug of home too strongly. Besides, now that he was a major, he had to turn his back on the Naughty Nineties and assume responsibility for his womenfolk. Once he had returned to South Africa, his older sister Anne – who had meanwhile qualified as a nurse in Bloemfontein – could commence her five years at the Royal Free Hospital in London, and then at the others of the few institutions which admitted women – in Cambridge, Edinburgh and Glasgow. By 1905, having missed the war, she could set herself up in private practice in Yeoville, Johannesburg. Under Dr C. Louis Leipoldt she would become the country's first ever woman school inspector of health, and a notable South African in her own right.

After London, Reggie's career is sufficiently clear from what follows for only a few extra details to be filled in here. In his autobiography Nathan chaffs his 'Reg', the now ardent republican – who came back not to the Free State, but to President Kruger's Transvaal – to occupy chambers in Marais Court in downtown Johannesburg. At first he had so little work that he had to borrow to pay the rent. In August, 1898, Smuts appointed him Second State Prosecutor there, and Nathan remembers fondly how Reg introduced the two of them for the first time. Indeed, the *Staatsalmanak der Zuid Afrikaansche Republiek* of 1898 lists only three new advocates admitted to the High Court around and after the Jameson Raid: Cleaver and Smuts (as State Prosecutor) in 1895, Reitz in 1897. From here date the jokes about the 'Augean stables' of our own Sodom and Gomorrah, with its corrupt police, tales of iniquitous crime and the folderol over illicit liquor and that Ontucht Wet devised to curb the rampant White Slave Traffic. (Reportedly Johannesburg centre had no less than 300 houses of ill fame, with 1 200 known prostitutes.) As the satirist Douglas Blackburn remarked (in *Life: A Subtropical Journal* on 4 March, 1899) of the Volksraad's attempt to clean up, "Sunday in Johannesburg was a day of much swearing and law-breaking and tomorrow will see hundreds of orgies in private rooms." There was the notorious Edgar Case, over a Zarp who hunted down and shot a British citizen in the sanctity of his own home, which, when he was lightly sentenced, resulted in an Uitlander petition for redress against

Introduction 21

official prejudice made to Queen Victoria herself. Reggie steered well clear of the Reform Committee, was becoming a people's hero of *The Standard and Diggers' News* and for his pains had the family residence firebombed.

What is not revealed in the documents here is that, once a state of war was declared between the Transvaal and Great Britain after the Ultimatum of 9 October, 1899, conscientious Reggie had the foresight to make his last will and testament. To this day it is preserved alongside his grandmother's, in the National Archives in Pretoria, together with his death notice, filed by his mother only on 24 June, 1902. The will of Veldcornet Cleaver is dated 16 December, 1899 – he had just had his birthday and would not live out his twenty-ninth year. He simply left all, including his copyrights, to his mother, should he predecease her (or otherwise to his two spinster sisters). Once the war was over and Marguerite was able to wind up the estate, she inherited and was able to pay off the cottage as her own. She refunded one R. Fenton, then of Colorado, a £650 loan advanced to Reggie before the war. She was obliged to auction off

Reggie's law books and most of his furniture, his horse and his bicycle (she kept his writing table and chair). Cash returned to her from Ceylon amounted to £44. 16s. 10d., out of which she repaid a certain Miss Ethel Smith the £24 which she had deposited for safekeeping for Reggie in the Banque Française (one may make of this extremely suggestive detail what one may – the Kroonstad crisis on p. 8 explained and a promised engagement, a planned escape to a French isle?). Marguerite was left with an estate valued at £2 057. 5s. 1d., which was certainly sufficient to see her through.

Also in the National Archives in Pretoria is the account of Commandant Koos Jooste (preserved in a German translation and later published), which records the day by day progress of that little publicised incident of the war, the Prieska invasion of February and March, 1900. Jooste's version correlates well with Reggie's one given here and assigns to him the dashing leadership role which he was too modest to advertise himself. Reggie's account perforce remains vague on details, as he wrote it while still at war, not wishing to incriminate any of his fellow burghers. The

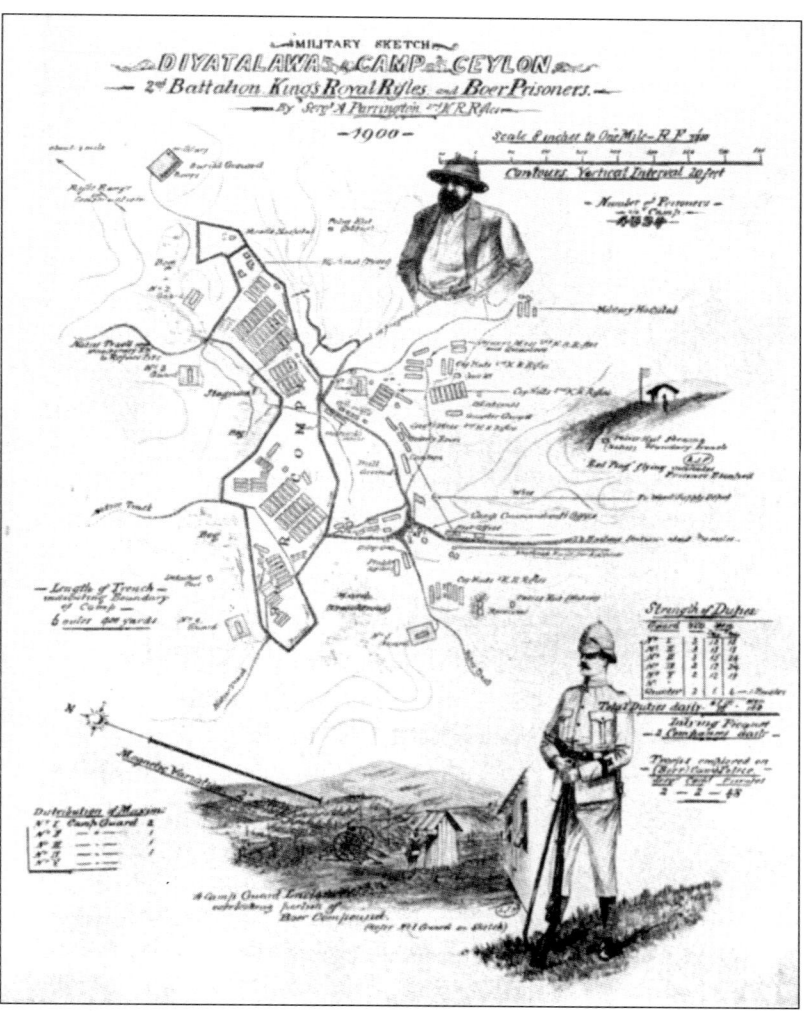

A map of Diyatalawa camp

An open-air kitchen at Diyatalawa

great adventure of his trek across enemy terrain back to Fourteen Streams, that tip of Transvaal soil just over the border at Warrenton where he was temporarily safe again, must also be read as presented with great discretion, so as not to offend the military reader over his shoulder. In the event, we realise, such subtle pleas for sympathy with the Boer cause were suppressed until hostilities ceased.

I still needed to gather material to fill in Marguerite de Fenton's compilation of the life of Reggie Cleaver. That meant consulting the Museum of the Anglo-Boer Wars in Bloemfontein, where Elria Wessels proved especially helpful. In their garden of remembrance his name is one of those inscribed on the plinth of the monument commemorating those Boer fighters who died in exile while in captivity, to one side from the names of thousands of others who perished closer to their own homes. The museum's photographic holdings include numerous pictures of the Green Point sorting camp enclosed on the cycle track, and of the camps in the south of Ceylon, particularly the largest one reserved for Free Staters in the mountains at dread Diyatalawa. Thanks to the

A bathing party at Diyatawala (courtesy MuseuMAfrica, Johannesburg)

Introduction 27

sheer boredom of year after year of internment, there the hobby of kodaking was permitted to flourish. Camp photographers lined up every activity before the lens – road-building parties (paid), religious revival services, the creepers growing over lanes between endless barracks, offices and stores, the three-legged race and the tug-of-war (OFS vs. Transvaal), the debating society and the kitchens, the bathing parties allowed in the jungle glades, the first hospital ward and the inevitable wooden white Celtic crosses in bleak ranks in the cemetery on a desolate slope.

Off Bowling Alley there was Wilhelmina Square, the Hollanders' quarter. The broken-nosed Anglo-Irish lightweight boxing champion of South Africa, Jim Holloway, posed with his pets, the Long Toms, their sleeves rolled up to their armpits, trained and ready to go the rounds for a purse (in rupees). The volunteer teachers of languages were inspanned for a group portrait, with their school bell.

After photography, the craze to pass the time was devising newspapers. Several were in English, presumably so as to flatter and tickle the regimental staff shipped in to guard them,

*One of several handmade newspapers
(courtesy National Archives, Pretoria)*

Introduction

also dying like flies in the heat. Apart from *De Krijgsgevangene* and *De Prikkeldraad*, among others there were *The Diyatalawa Camp Lyre* and *The Diyatalawa Dum-Dum*. The latter begins with an explanation that 'diya' was the Sinhalese for water-spring and 'talawa' meant rolling valleys as far as the eye could see. Vol. 1, No. 1, of the *Dum-Dum* of 10 September, 1900, is handwritten and com-mences with an ingratiating editorial:

> ... In a community such as ours, so much depends on those placed in authority over us, and if our Fate was unkind in sending us against our will to see the beauties of Ceylon, she has relented in placing us under humane officers and gentlemen...

Among the advertisements for Professor Fraser's Palmistry (Hut 11) and the Happy Valley Beer-Hall (Hut 15), there is a column-stopping poem called "In Exile", a nostalgic evocation of their home beyond the sea, the sea which most of them had never seen before: "The dear dead voices of the veld awake... The might have been."

Occupants of Hut 27, Diyatalawa
(courtesy Museum of the Anglo-Boer Wars, Bloemfontein)

Even amateur drama criticism was now practised. After one Saturday evening in the Recreation Hall a broadsheet was published to commend the production by Mr A. P. Roos's company of the play, *Lotgevallen der Voortrekkers*, performed before a packed audience. Roos himself gave an exceptionally clever imitation of a Zulu war dance, while C. J. van Rooyen's sympathetic impersonation of Letty well merited the rounds of applause.

Another handout read as follows:

> Inhabitants of the Camp will be glad to learn that the gong, from which Camp time is now taken, is under orders for removal to Band quarters for tuning. Scale suggested by several correspondents – B flat.

As if presenting themselves in their best for a census, the occupants of each hut, from old takhaars to very young bucks, under solatopis with their pipes, posed time and again before tripods. Even the line-up of Reggie's Hut 27, caught after he had died, is preserved on record. His funeral, however – with him wrapped in the Vierkleur, and sent off with a huge demonstration of silent protest – was not filmed. The MuseuMAfrica in Johannesburg (not to mention many other holdings) also has a fine selection of these unique images of human endurance and crestfallen patience from Diyatalawa, together with some heart-rending scenes back at Braamfontein station.

Apart from Brink's record, surprisingly little of such prisoner of war experience is readily and publicly available in English. There is Ben Viljoen's *My Reminiscences of the Anglo-Boer War*, written to pass the days and the censor at Saint Helena in 1902. Then there is only Victor Pohl's *Adventures of a Boer Family* (1944), recalling how he acquired a fiddle to cheer up his compatriots at Green Point. But of Diyatalawa and the other camps in British Ceylon and over on mainland India there is little recollection other than Reggie's brief and forced, rather chipper documents, written to reassure his desperate kinsfolk. Nor was I sure that, in studying the official necrology of Diyatalawa Camp, I was getting behind Reggie's words to the true agony of such a talented and principled person, pulling against his only support – his mother, his enemy.

In August, 1995, I went to the independent

country of Sri Lanka. At the suggestion of Karel Schoeman, I hunkered down in their Department of National Archives in Colombo 7. Between times I walked along the palm-fringed coral beaches to Mount Lavinia, used as a recuperation ward for those prisoners of war (and now a luxury resort). I entrained for Galle, where the Dutch East India Co. erected a five-pointed, enormously ramparted castle as well, from which to ship slaves, spices and seed, their VOC monogram on glassware and on branded human flesh. Such a haunting irony I would not have imagined without seeing it: one ex-Dutch entrepot receiving the descendants of another Dutch entrepot along the route, all soon under British sway.

At Kandy the hard-labour prison of Ragama for recalcitrants, and the extension at Urugasmanhandiya, now obliterated. At Kanattha in the Anglican section the graves of the fallen, still well tended: names like Leon Kock (the seventeen year old grandson of the general beaten at Elandslaagte), Joubert, Massyn, Smuts, Frederick Scott (who died in the Mental Asylum), Nel, Foley ... Rust in Vrede, Overl. te Selon ... In the National Museum, a display of handmade curios like the ones back in Bethlehem.

Back in the archives, alongside gracious monks in saffron robes and sandals deciphering sacred texts in the thousand year old Buddhist language of Pali. Surely I was the only Westerner in a very long time to be summoning up the accounts of those bedraggled thousands, who were not treated cruelly and neglected, but just moved aside... whispering for assistance, bowing my head; fingering a frangipani blossom, a bit tearful. In the distance the spitting sound of a machine-gun – *their* civil war.

Soon I tumbled on the splendid tale of H. E. Engelbrecht, the last of those bittereinders who held out for over a year longer, refusing to take the oath of loyalty to King Edward VII. The camp was eventually closed on him; he was discharged and, because he was such a fine marksman, given the post of controlling poaching as Warden of the Yala Game Sanctuary (where he died in 1922).

Then I found 'Sister Lucy', whose comforting words of condolence close this work with a terrible agony. She was an older, disinterested Englishwoman who, on hearing of the plight of the Boer prisoners in the Indian Ocean, had the determination to get up a small staff of

Introduction 35

trainee nurses and sail out to assist. Only their surnames are known: Gregson, von Dadelesen, Gray, Baldwin. Like Mary Kingsley, they volunteered, without payment, to serve their country's defeated foes. Sister Lucy had immediately to beat the measles outbreak and then bring under control the virulent epidemic of enteric fever, introduced by a batch of Boer captives arrived on the transport *S. S. Bavarian*. To a ward for 25 she had to annex huts for an additional 280 beds. Out of the 602 cases of typhoid – the peak being reached in November, 1900, when 370 new ones occurred – there were 50 deaths in all, aged from 16 to 90. Reggie was one of those. They had carved their own crosses.

By January, 1901, she could report in *The Ceylon Review*:

> We are working under Burgher doctors, very decent men. One I like very much. Truly the Boers are very pleasant to nurse. You do not hear bad language or at least very little, and never a bad remark or expression, or even a look, so that in all this crowd of men I can safely allow my fair young nurses to go

> with me. Having nursed my own countrymen, alas! the difference is perceptible...

Every researcher in this strange backwater area of that long-running South African war is indebted to two figures: their names are Lewis and Brohier. The first was Mr J. Penry Lewis of the Ceylon Civil Service who in 1913 – knowing nothing of Marguerite's efforts – was stationed up on the scenic railway at Diyatalawa. His antiquarian pastime was to collect material for his great work of history, *Tombstones and Monuments of Ceylon*. Hence the sketch of Reggie's primitive tomb with its coiling lilies, reproduced here, and with its reference to Psalm 116, Verse 7 ("Return unto thy rest, O my soul: for the Lord has dealt bountifully with thee"). Its misspelt 'Mostin' indicates that, when he was known by that name, it was in the English pronunciation. Soon that parade ground of graves was to be ploughed over, the roll-call of the dead being transferred to a stone obelisk, now in the care of the Commonwealth War Graves Commission. Reggie's name is on the northern face, overlooking a Lankan Buddhist temple and

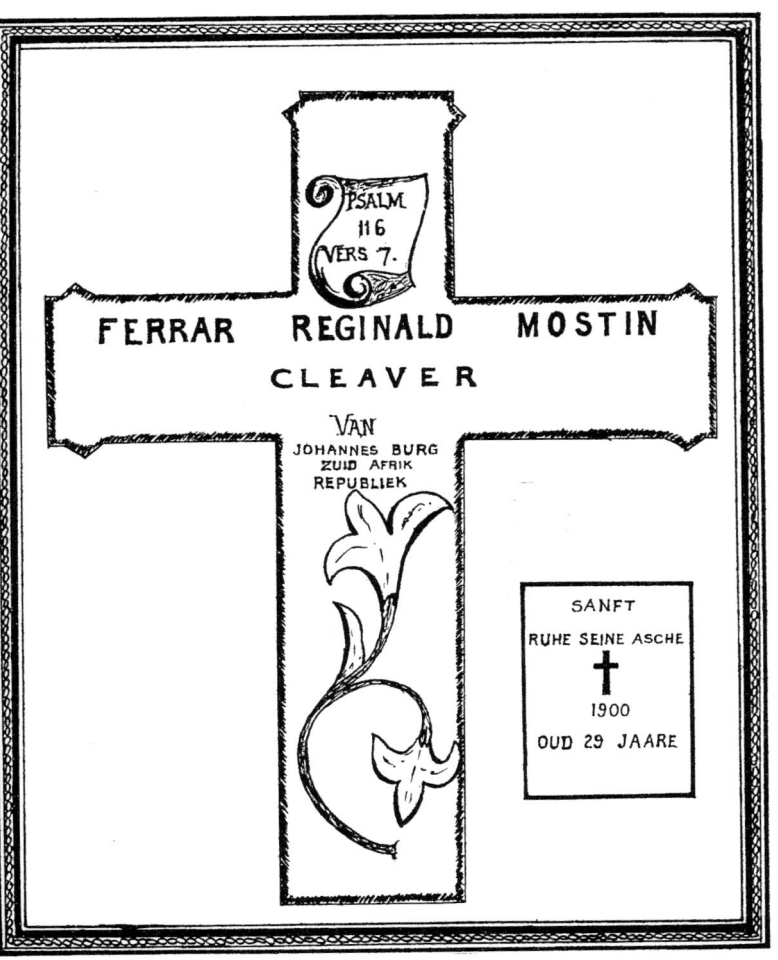

*The Lewis sketch of Reggie's grave
(courtesy of National Archives, Pretoria)*

The cemetery at Diyatalawa after the typhoid epidemic

Introduction 39

surrounded by lemon-scented grass and syringas.

The other man who made it his life's work to record each and every detail of the presence of the Boer prisoners in Ceylon was Dr R. L. Brohier, F. R. G. S. In *The Journal of the Dutch Burgher Union of Ceylon*, published in Colombo, from Vol. 36, No. 1 of July, 1946, to Vol. 37, No. 4 of April, 1947, he placed the nine instalments of his account (with an addendum by L. G. Poulier in Vol. 38 in the following July). Brohier simply recuperated all the data there was about that extraordinary event in the island's memory, the arrival of shipload after shipload of shaggy prisoners, Reggie an officer among them, and then their sensational departure two and more years later. Over those who did not return to South Africa, with admirable devotion – and on behalf of that other Burgher community there, half belonging to the conquerors and half conquered themselves – he kept the flame.

As the reader of these *War Letters* will realise, Reggie died quicker than the communication network of the day could alert his loved ones. Even the conservative *South Africa* noted with regret the death of Advocate R. M. Cleaver among Boer prisoners of meningitis and enteric, but over two months late (on 19 January, 1901). Many of the letters were first read only some years after he drafted them and as a voice from the grave.

When *A Young South African* was at last published, in its beautiful first edition, and distributed by Hortor selling at 7/6 a copy – it should also be noted – *The South African Bookman* of March, 1914, took it up, listing it as their 'Book of the Quarter.' That was an appropriate tribute to a South African classic of its kind in the making.

STEPHEN GRAY.

Johannesburg,
      November, 2000.

SELECT BIBLIOGRAPHY

Brink, J. N., *Recollections of a Boer Prisoner-of-War at Ceylon*, Amsterdam/Cape Town: Hollandsch-Afrikaansche Uitgevers-Maatschappij/Jac. Dusseau & Co., 1904.

de Villiers, W. M., "Hierdie Brit was 'n Boer", *Die Huisgenoot*, 17 November, 1950, pp. 33–35.

Gray, Stephen, "Dead Man's Disclosure", *Gabriel's Exhibition*, Cape Town: Mayibuye, 1998, pp. 81–84.

Groenewald, Coen, *Bannelinge oor die Oseaan: Boerekrygsgevangenes (1899–1902)*, Pretoria: J. P. van der Walt, 1992.

Leipoldt, C. Louis, "Lewensskets: Dr Anne Cleaver", *Die Huisgenoot*, 23 January, 1923, pp. 366–8.

Macnab, Roy, "The English Burghers", *News/check*, 17 April, 1970, p. 29–31.

42 Select Bibliography

Nathan, Manfred, *Not Heaven Itself: An Autobiography*, Durban: Knox, 1944.

Reitz, F. W., "Lewensskets: Veldkornet F. R. Mostyn Cleaver", *Die Huisgenoot*, March, 1923, pp. 464–6.

Entries for F. R. M. Cleaver in the *Standard Encyclopedia of Southern Africa*, Vol. 3 (1971) and the *Dictionary of South African Biography*, Vol. 3 (1977); for Marguerite de Fenton in *Companion to South African English Literature* (1986). See also *A Dictionary of South African English* (1996).

PREFACE

HIS little book is one of many tokens of a mother's love. It represents a collection of her beloved son's letters made by a lady of more than fourscore years who is, nevertheless, to the joy of all who are privileged to know her, still in possession of all her original vigour of mind and strength of character. But the book is something more. It is the record of some of the experiences of one who, in no mere conventional sense, was a friend, and made a deep and abiding impress upon all with whom he came in contact. His untimely death is mourned by all with whom he had to do, fellow students and colleagues at the Bar, comrades on commando, and Court officials, pressmen, and policemen. They need no incentive to keep his memory green. But a wider public may wish to know more of one who was a true South African, loyal to the

land of his birth, sincerely anxious to contribute towards making his people respected among the nations, a fighter for truth, a lover of mankind.

It would be out of place to attempt a formal biography. All that need be done is to set down a few plain facts to give continuity to the narrative which follows, framed as it is almost entirely in his own words.

Ferrar Reginald Mostyn Cleaver was the son of English parents who settled in the Orange Free State at a time when lions still snatched unwary girls from the drinking places, when the " New Rush " was undreamt of, and the young Republics were struggling in debt and surrounded by savage enemies.

"Dick," as he was known to his intimates (though his relatives called him " Reg ") was born at Zuringkrans, in the district of Bethlehem, on the 12th December 1870. He grew up like any farmer's son, and loved the open, free life of the veld and the berg, learned to ride and to shoot, and, what is not always so common an accomplishment, to speak the truth. The earliest formative inflence was that of his mother, who found the time, in the midst of her household duties, to give the

Preface ix

first direction to many who were to become distinguished Free Staters in after times. He then went to St. Andrew's School at Bloemfontein, where he first wrestled with Arnold's "Latin Prose Composition" and other works of an equally terrifying nature. This was a school conducted on the lines of the best Church of England traditions, and under the guidance of its head master "Dick" Cleaver made excellent progress. In due time he proceeded to Grey College, then under the headship of Dr. Brill, whose favourite pupil he became. His old principal says of him that he was distinguished not more by his devotion to his studies than by his instant appreciation of what was good and noble. At the Grey College Cleaver matriculated and obtained a State exhibition, tenable for three years. He then went to England and entered as a law student at the Middle Temple. Here he found himself not only in the broad atmosphere of English legal life, but in the congenial society and comradeship of the young South African students, with whom he formed fast friendships which were to endure to the end of his days.

That he devoted time to his studies was evidenced by the fact that he gained prizes at the Inns of Court, one of them being the Equity Scholarship. At the same time he was learning much from the open book of life around him. He went to Holland and learned the language, retaining ever after something of the Netherlands twang when addressing juries in Cape Dutch. To France and Germany he went in student fashion, returning to complete his course for the Bar, to which he was called in June 1892.

At first he had thoughts of remaining in London, and he might have made for himself an English career had he done so. He was one of the counsel briefed for the defence in the trial of the Tower Hill anarchists, in which great public interest was taken, for at this time the anarchists loomed large in the general eye. He also appeared for the defence in the prosecution of Fritz Brall, known as the Chelsea Explosives Case. Two such introductions as these would have sufficed to presage fame in the case of most Old Bailey men; but Cleaver decided to return to South Africa, and in 1895 he was admitted as an advocate of the South African Republic. He began practice at Johannesburg, and soon obtained a considerable

Preface

amount of support. He made a home for his aged mother and himself at Yeoville, and became a popular member of the Rand Club.

At this period great things were happening. The Jameson Raid threw all South Africa into a ferment, and men began to range themselves on one side or the other. The London student days had seen the formation of a Young Afrikander party, the leading figures in which were de Villiers, Hertzog, and Smuts. To these Cleaver had attached himself by the strongest ties. Though of English parentage, he was born and brought up in a Boer republic, and it was to a great extent natural that he should feel greater love for the country of his boyhood and youth. He admired what was best in the English character, but at the same time he ardently desired to maintain the dearly bought independence of his homeland; and in the Raid he saw the menace of a forbidding future. These Young Afrikanders were enlightened, and they saw the need for reform in the body politic. But that reform they felt must come from within. While they desired to preserve their national flag and all that it meant to them, they were filled with a determination to weed out the evils caused by an effete oligarchy, and to use all the influence at their command towards the establishment of a pure and honest administration which should win the respect of burghers and uitlanders alike.

Imbued with these ideas, Cleaver readily, in 1898, accepted the offer made to him by Jan Smuts, then State Attorney of the South African Republic, that he should become Second State Prosecutor for the Witwatersrand. The Augean Stable at Johannesburg needed much cleansing. The trade in illicit liquor and the White Slave traffic were in a flourishing condition. Many of the officials, including no inconsiderable number of the police, were in the pay of publicans and procurers. Even some Volksraad members were not free from the taint, and on occasion jurymen did not go unbribed. Cleaver set himself resolutely to eradicate the blight. There was only a limited number of officials whom he could trust, and they had to fight enemies in their own ranks. But Cleaver "stood up to it" manfully, and in time his energy, untiring zeal, and scorn of consequence met with their reward. He had filled his office but eighteen months when war came, but during that brief time he had contributed much towards infusing a new spirit into administrative matters. He was just the type of man the Transvaal needed for the cure of its soul, and, unfortunately for South Africa, he went too soon. His career, brief as it was, remains a lesson and an inspiration to his compatriots.

It is impossible in cold print to describe his personality. In appearance he was somewhat awkward, with long lanky figure, and arms that tossed about like those of a windmill when he was in Court. But there was a fire in his eye, an alertness in his face, that told of a strong spirit within. He was, as may be imagined, no mollycoddle, and loved to shoot, or ride, or fight, as well as any man. He was always cheery until near the end, and loved a practical joke, and he was full of those rough witticisms which are born of the veld and the open air.

The remainder of his brief story is told in the narrative which follows, constructed partly by his mother, and partly from his own letters. It has an interest of its own, not merely as an account of his experiences during an interesting phase of the great Boer War, but as the revelation of a character which is all too rare.

He rests in a distant island, but his memory abides with us. It has been a melancholy pleasure, as well as a great privilege, for me to have been asked to contribute a few words to this memorial of him.

       MANFRED NATHAN.

Johannesburg,
  June 1913.

A Young South African

CHAPTER I

WAR CLOUDS

HE question of his nationality was long pending. His parents were and the remaining one, his mother, continues wholeheartedly British. Yet being born and reared in the Orange Free State he had the right to choose to which he would belong, the country of his descent, or that of his birth. Had it not been for the troubles in the Transvaal, the question would never have come into prominence. He would have lived his life, proud of his British blood, but sincerely attached to his native land.

But in '97-8 the lines began to draw strongly apart between Boer and Briton; yet still the chances of war were not so marked as to be perceived, except by the few on both sides who were determined it should come. To him it seemed more a question of reform in the administration of justice and of equal rights. Feeling strongly on these points, and advised thereto by his trusted friend and counsellor

Dr. J. Farrelly, he accepted in 1898 the post of Second Public Prosecutor in Johannesburg, which entailed his becoming a Burgher of the Transvaal.

You know that I was not only willing, but pleased that he should take the post. There was crying need of a man like him, incorruptible, fearless, and unsparing of personal work. The only part of it I disliked was the acceptance of the Transvaal Burgher Right. It separated him definitely from my country and was a wrench to me. My compensation was, the knowledge that he would be doing good and sorely needed work. Little did I foresee the terrible lengths to which his duty would call him.

But in certain quarters his appointment gave great umbrage. He met with anything but a cordial reception in the department, or a smooth path. Every step was watched and scrutinized in order to find something against him.

He was reported to Pretoria as having spoken unprofessionally of his Superiors in the Department; but Jan Smuts, the State Attorney, stood faithfully by him.

The police were through and through the reverse of what he desired, and were against him to a man. He had been appointed with an authority entirely independent, but was galled by interference, and a continual reference to himself as "my assistant." When all these things failed to move him, he was, under cover of a request for amicable help, crushed with work, properly belonging to others. Night after night he sat in his office at home, working at these things until midnight—one—two—or three o'clock in the morning. Punctually at nine a.m. he must be at the Court.

The first case he tackled, with all the determination of his character, was the making of the Morality Law a Living Power, instead of, as it had hitherto remained, a Dead Letter. This was a fight to the death with—it is not too much to say—the Devil and all his angels. He was thwarted on every side by mysterious agencies of which he well knew the source. All his plans for securing the criminals were futile. He was offered enormous bribes to discontinue his pursuit; these failing he was threatened with the alternative of "shooting irons"; but he persevered and after many weeks got a conviction and sentence against the principal criminal, one Joe Silver.

At the same time trainloads of Silver's victims were sent over the border to Cape Town. The geographical conditions of the Transvaal rendered the Government powerless to send them further.

Silver was condemned to two years' imprisonment with hard labour—he deserved hanging—but a few weeks after his incarceration he was pardoned. Only himself and one other knew why. Not long after, he fell under the law for a still more heinous crime.

This is the remark of the "Leader" upon the matter:

"Mr. Justice Esser has sentenced the ruffian Silver to two years of hard labour in prison, with expulsion from the State at the end of that time. It is a lenient sentence. We dare not publish the evidence that was heard by the Judge and jury; it was too revolting for a public page, and though Mr. Cleaver, by the skill of his cross-examination, succeeded in showing the utter corruption of the police, we cannot help him by the detailed exposure of the facts, elicited by his questions.

"Until Mr. Mostyn Cleaver took this foul thing in both hands, and crushed it in the head, no one dared move. He has risked his position, his character, and his life, and we must give him every sort of praise for his courage."

After winning the "Silver Case" he prosecuted in the "Mrs. Robinson Enquiry."

This was an investigation as to the cause of the death of a Mrs. Robinson, which was alleged to have occurred through taking medicine carelessly prepared. This was a very important enquiry and interesting from the medical and scientific points raised, as to whether the symptoms revealed by the post-mortem were those of poisoning or ptomaines.

The body had been buried some weeks before exhumation for the post-mortem.

Every physician in town gave evidence. The

conduct of the prosecution was an immense strain. His own health was at this time under the daily supervision of his friend Dr. Rogers, who was also of very great service to him in coaching him in the medical evidence.

The trial resulted in the acquittal of the doctor charged.

Another important prosecution was the trial of Jones for the shooting of Edgar, which made a great noise at the time and contributed much to the crisis.

Jones was one of the town police. Upon a certain night Edgar got into a street row and knocked a man down with such force, that the fellow lay stunned on the road.

Edgar then entered his dwelling and, it being late, prepared to go to bed, his wife and children being in the house with him.

Jones meanwhile came up with another policeman, knocking at the door for admission. Edgar took no notice but continued undressing. Jones then forced the door, whilst his assistant did the same to the window.

As Jones entered, Edgar met him with, it was affirmed, a stick, which Jones's excitement magnified into a bar of iron. Whereupon, anticipating the attack of Edgar, Jones fired and his revolver ball passed through Edgar's heart, causing instantaneous death.

Jones was arrested, and in the preliminary examination the charge was reduced to manslaughter and Jones let out on a small bail.

6   A Young South African

Instantly Johannesburg was up in arms. A monster meeting was called in the Market Place to protest.

This meeting was illegal. The law said that not more that twelve persons might come together in any public place, and these might not deliver speeches.

More than a thousand persons met on this occasion, including some carriages in which were the female relatives of some of the leaders, who waved flags and cheered. Speeches of no very moderate tone were delivered. The police were not very far off, however, and the meeting was dispersed, the speechmakers being arrested.

Although the law forbade open-air assemblies, those in a building were not included in the prohibition. So a meeting was convened for the following Saturday in the Amphitheatre, a building capable of holding some thousands.

The building was crowded to suffocation. But when the speakers mounted the platform and began, they could get no further than "Gentlemen." All the cries of the street and the gallery arose to drown the voices of the orators. Again and again they tried; but each time the uproar became more deafening. Then amid the babel was heard an ominous sound of breaking wood. This was followed by a general rush for the platform, with a waving of broken chair legs, which were employed to such purpose that the Amphitheatre was quickly cleared, though not without many broken heads. The place had been quietly filled with low class Dutch before the meeting began.

The police present remained passive, refusing to interfere when appealed to, but enjoyed the scene with much laughter. Not only this, but several minor officials took an active part in the fray as well as in its organization.

This event was followed by the monster petition to the Queen, signed by twenty-one thousand Uitlanders, which, together with the Jones-Edgar affair, became a powerful weapon in the hands of Britain.

The further conduct of this celebrated trial was committed to my son.

On the last day of the trial he said to me: "Mother, if you like, you may come and hear the conclusion."

He stated the case clearly and strongly, and demonstrated from authorities in English Courts that a policeman cannot, without a warrant, force an entrance into a house, and asked for a conviction.

The Judge summed up and charged the jury overwhelmingly in favour of the prisoner, denying altogether any weight to the authorities quoted by the Public Prosecutor. Although such precedents were always admitted in these Courts, they were only English law, he said, and not applicable here.

The prisoner was acquitted.

In coming out of Court my son remarked to

me emphatically: "We have not heard the last of this. The Judge has knocked a big nail into our coffin to-day."

The strain of official work, joined to a very poignant private anxiety, was telling grievously upon his health. His nerves were always abnormally highstrung, "lying upon the top of his skin." His appetite, usually so healthy, fell off; he could not sleep. Going one morning into his room before he was up, his bedroom clock lay crushed upon the floor. Its ticking, during the night, had wrought him to fury, and he had dashed his boot at it to stop its noise.

Usually so cheerful and sociable he, about this time, entreated me to forego our little gatherings of musical friends. He would rise from the almost untasted dinner, and go out on the hill-side in darkness, or rain, there to wander over the veld, seeking to calm his tortured nerves.

An overmastering desire for solitude seized him. He must be alone. Every sound, even the turning of the page of a book; every sight, even of persons the most dear, jarred horribly. He fell ill. It was a near run with death. As soon as he was able to move, Dr. Rogers ordered him away. He went down to Kroonstad, and I begged of him to try to settle there one great matter that was troubling him.

He returned after a few days much better, but with his private difficulty still unsolved, and still a prey to profound melancholy. He must, he *would* be alone. I must go away for a month at least, and leave him to fight it out alone, or he should go mad. As this opinion was strongly backed by his doctor, I very reluctantly, with many tears and a sorely wounded heart, left him.

His letters during my absence were most affectionate. At the end of the month I wrote, saying I had a mind to remain another month. The following letter was his reply:

> Rand Club,
> Johannesburg.
> S. A. R.
> Aug. 2nd 1899.

My dearest Mother,

I want you to come back as soon as you can. The reason is, that the supreme desire of my heart, for so long past, is realized. My dear Sophie has consented to marry me, and before very long we shall be joined.

In the meanwhile I want you, my dearest old mother, to spend with me the remaining short period of my bachelorhood. After that you can go to the Orange Free State for such time as we may arrange upon, or settle for the future in any other way we may think best. I do not intend to wait long for the final step; not more than a few weeks.

On Friday night I am going down to Kroonstad. I should very much like to be here to receive you on your return; but owing to the next circuit Court opening on Tuesday, I shall be unable to go down for some time to come, unless I go now, and that would not leave me sufficient time to make the arrangements necessary before I marry. I shall be back on Tuesday morning.

I am so supremely happy, Mother, that I can scarcely realize this sudden revulsion. I feel as if I were in one moment rescued from the quicksand of intellectual torpor.

The bottomless sea of utter apathy which for some time past has held me, seems to have suddenly terminated in a pleasant shore, where there is health and vigour, and where God's World is good to look upon; where one fights his Battles with an interest other than that of the scientific expert, who fights for the sake of his science only.

Do not think that in my new joys I shall love you the less, but rather the more.

With best love to you, my dearest Mother,
Your affectionate son,
(signed) REG.

This marriage, however, never took place, owing to circumstances upon which we will keep silence.

To return. The troubles of the times began to come to a head. The Press duel between the "Leader" and "Standard and Diggers" became fiercer. Every one had to choose his side—Republics or Empire. More than one appeal I received to use my influence to bring him to the latter. But I knew it would be in vain to try. However he might have hesitated in the choice of his nationality, once it was decided, it became a point of honour with him to be true to that side to which he had sworn allegiance.

His one answer to the arguments of his many friends on the side of the Empire was: "It is a point of honour, I cannot draw back from the obligations I have undertaken to the Republic, now that she is rushing upon deadly peril."

To me his unfailing reply was: "Mother, England is *your* country, you are right to abide by her; Africa is mine, and it is my duty to stand by her."

"But, my dear son, your blood is English; all your family, most of your friends are British."

"Yes, Mother, *that* is the hard part of it. But Africa is my native land, in spite of my English blood."

"If it were possible for the Republics to win this war, or to destroy Britain, have you ever reflected what that would mean to the whole human race? What barrier would remain against the tyrants of the world?"

"O Mother, I know that England has more freedom, and better laws and institutions, but if they would give us time and chance, we will make Africa as good and free as Britain. The old generation can't live for ever. But if war comes, as seems only too likely, I shall be found on the side of Africa. If my country must suffer, I will suffer with her."

People had now begun to send away their families to Durban, the Cape, or England. Every departing train was full.

Government began to tighten the reins upon the Press. Some of the more obnoxious editors took timely departure. The editor of the "Leader" was arrested on his way down to the station. The sub-editor escaped owing to a timely warning. When October 1899 opened, a panic seized the population. Ordinary trains were no longer sufficient. Only first class tickets were issued, but every class, and even open trucks, were filled with the fleeing crowd. The numbers rose from five hundred to eight, ten, twelve hundred, and in the last day or two to fifteen and eighteen hundred in each train.

My son wished me to go to London. But nothing short of bodily force would have induced me to leave Johannesburg whilst he remained. My life was at that time one huge anxiety. He had by now seen plainly what the end would be, and asked me to lay in stores for the coming need. Most people bought only for a month, or at the most two. Boers knew exactly the unpreparedness of the British and reckoned upon a rapid descent upon Durban, which they thought would bring the foe to his knees. Britain, at least as represented in Africa, thought the first battle (they meant to have a decisive victory) would leave the Republics in their hands.

"Mother, both are wrong. Lay in stores for a year at least."

Well it was that I did so.

We tried to hope for a peaceful settlement, even whilst preparing for the worst. But it was a gloomy, anxious time. He tried to inspire me with courage to face the worst. "You ought to be like the Spartan mothers and inspire me."

"No, no, I would not give you, even if by so doing I could save the State."

But he was not indifferent to my trouble. We were sitting one evening on the Stoep after dinner, according to our custom. He sat on the step silently thinking. I knew he was weighing my anxiety against his inclination and duty as a citizen. I sat down beside him and put my arms round him: "My dear, dear boy! Do not go to the front, whatever happens. Think! If you fall, you leave three women desolate. You are the only man left to your sisters and myself in the world."

"O Mother, Mother, do not make it harder for me than it is. It is hard enough to leave you. Help me rather to do my duty."

In these last days before the fatal decision for war, he was active in using such influence as he possessed to do good turns to any who required them. British residents leaving had to abandon property the loss of which meant in many cases ruin. Then he would obtain a permit for one of the Firm to remain, to protect, as far as possible, their interests; or it might be a case of poverty or sickness, which made the reaching of a place of refuge impossible; or again, goods or animals would be commandeered; but the requisition notes, but for his intervention, would have been withheld.

On the 9th October all hope passed away with the dispatch of the Ultimatum.

The rush from the town became frantic. I wished to remain in our cottage at Yeoville, but he decided that I must not risk that in the prevailing uncertainty. Whilst communication was still open, telegrams passed between him and his close friend, which resulted in my taking up my quarters in the doctor's house, a step that placed me under the direct protection of the Chief Detective, whose office was just across the street, and also was the salvation of the valuable premises and effects of the doctor.

I had written to the State Secretary, Mr. Reitz, an urgent appeal to prevent my son's going to the front. I stated his bodily disabilities, also that being the only son of his Mother, and she a widow, the law of the commando especially provided for his exemption. This was not without effect.

As soon as he volunteered for the front, it was represented to him that his services as Veldcornet of the Southern division of the town would be more valuable to the State than his single rifle. So he accepted the position.

War Clouds

It was he who drew up the regulations of Rust-en-Orde and organized the Special Police. It soon became apparent that notwithstanding the immense clearance of the Kafirs from the mines great numbers had secreted themselves. These were only discovered by night explorations, which he personally undertook.

Much more dangerous, as he often said, were these expeditions than the open field. He succeeded in capturing the Kafir beer and arms which they were secretly making in the deserted mines, and in putting thousands of the natives across the Portuguese border, thus removing the greatest immediate danger to the town.

Not long after the commencement of the war the women raided Chinese shops for food.

It fell to him to pacify them, which with some difficulty he did. At first they were for tearing him limb from limb, as one of the "verfluckste" officials who had sent their husbands to commando and left them to starve. Yes! they would write to their husbands to come back and shoot these officials. But when the six foot six "verfluckste" answered all their rage with "grappijes" and merry laughter, offering himself a willing sacrifice to their rage, they could only find in their hearts to laugh with the merry youth. And when he led them to his office, and distributed orders for food and fuel, and then promised them regular weekly rations (a promise faithfully kept) they literally *hugged* him. Henceforth he became a hero to these poor women. All their troubles were brought to him. When, later on, he went to the front, many was the visit I had from one or other, entreating me: "Send for your son back again; nobody cares for us now he is gone!"

One night, after the death of General Kok, mortally wounded at Elandslaagte, and who died in Ladysmith, he came home in a white heat of indignation caused by the affidavits of certain persons who had been allowed to enter Ladysmith at the deceased General's request to attend him. "If such actions as these can be perpetrated by the British, nothing on earth shall keep me from the front. If I can do nothing else I can die revenging such atrocities."

Before long, however, they were brought to acknowledge that "they had let their lip wag a little too freely."

But other reports came from time to time, keeping up the excitement of the young men, as they were intended to do.

On 17 December he came to tell me he could no longer rest in town whilst others were dying at the front. He had got leave at last, in spite of my exertions to the contrary, to go to the front for one month only.

He chose the Western Army. He said he could not go to Natal because so many of his personal friends were in the I.L.H., which was fighting there. Another reason for going west was, that Commandant Ferreira was in chief command there, and he thought I should feel less anxiety, knowing him to be under so valued a friend of my own as he.

But anyway, his going was a terrible blow to me. He was my one and only protector, my all on earth most dear. I tried hard, but I knew uselessly, to turn his resolution. I told him, that now he was going the authorities would no longer leave me unmolested, knowing as they did my British nationality, and never concealed sympathies. He heard me in silence.

I packed his necessary kit, bedewing it with many tears unseen of him. Then I drove with him down to the station. It was Sunday morning the 17th of December. Most, if not all of the officials remaining in town were on the platform to see him off. Taking my hand, he said: "Here is my Mother. She is a British subject. She fears that when I am gone you will not treat her well. Whoever is my friend, will befriend my Mother. Whoever lifts a finger against her, will have me to reckon with on my return."

Turning to one who professed special obligations to him, he added laughingly: "You've got a revolver, old man; don't fear to use it for my Mother's protection. I'll take the consequences."

It is only justice to say that I enjoyed the most complete freedom of speech and action during his absence.

He entered the carriage amid handshakings and good wishes. The bell gave two solemn dirge-like tolls as the train moved off. It smote upon my heart like his death knell.

The letters he wrote me from the front continue his story.

A few months earlier he wrote the following letter to his uncle with reference to the trials already mentioned.

Rand Club, Johannesburg,
S. Africa,
May ½th L' ((1899.

My dear old Baas,

Be not afraid lest I have placed at the top of this letter some fearful and wonderful sign of the Secret Order of Assassins, or other kindred body. The fact is that I was writing the date and forgot to shift key.

It is long indeed since I wrote to you about myself and my doings; but I hope this time, if nothing intervenes, to bring to a conclusion a letter of wholly personal import. To begin with we are all well, though at Easter time Mother had a very bad attack of influenza and for awhile the Doctor almost gave her up. She is, however, now restored to health and in a fit condition to stand up against me in battle and defy my order against the performance of housework.

Your deponent, too, is in robust health, though he too, not long ago, was in a very bad state of overwork. A short holiday of ten days duration, however, cleared away the cobwebs, and once more all goes merrily as a marriage bell.

You must know, Old Warhorse, this yer brak

nigger he fell among thieves and villains; and he sprang upon the ruffians and choked them.

It was a game of kill or be killed; war to the knife, which I waged, in the first serious business I undertook in my official capacity (Know that my unworthiness is installed second Publiek Aanklager of Johannesburg, with a hand independent of the first ditto). You my old and faithful friend will, I know, be pleased to hear that I was signally successful. The enclosed cutting [quoted on page 4—Ed.] will likewise show you that my performance is esteemed a public benefit and that I am credited with full measure.

It came on this wise. You have doubtless heard of the Lexen Enquiry, which was held in New York a couple of years back. Many of the identical ruffians who were driven out then came here and quickly organized among us similar abuses.

Jan Smuts, our present Attorney General and Chief of our department, is a young man of my own age and of unimpeachable honour. He reorganized the department by placing in it men like Louis Jacobsz, Andreas Stockenstrom, and other young Afrikanders zealous for reform. His policy, firmly backed up by us, his subordinates, is " fiat justitia ruat coelum "—in the colloquial " stoot deur, al barst de bottel."

Now such an attitude you may conceive was regarded with no friendly eye by those against whose interests it militated, official or criminal;

but on the other hand it obtained for him the strong support of all right-minded Afrikanders and Uitlanders, by whom our Party is regarded as the Rising Hope.

True, they began by open scoffing at "this young Buster, with his department of Boys," but finished up by wholesomely dreading or straightforwardly hoping in him. He tackled many things and set them in order. He broke up one or two gangs, who stood in his path, and soon changed the ridicule into terror.

Now to come to my story. You must know that many branches of the law here in our jurisdiction on the Rand, were for long of none effect. It passed into a truism, that excellent laws were passed in the Rand for the eyes of the world, and to uphold abstract principles, but were never intended for concrete application. One of these was the Morality Law, called in Dutch the Ontucht Wet. It was nicknamed in punning mockery the Untouched Law, because, though the evil at whose extirpation it aimed was a crying one, it had never yet been more than a dead letter.

From the pages of the Lexen Enquiry, you will be familiar with the iniquitous combinations by which this law was made an engine of blackmail and organized villainy. Exactly the same state of things prevailed here. Mr. Smuts sent for me in December last and told me I must tackle the business (it had previously been in other hands).

War Clouds 21

I went into things and found that there were organized gangs of ruffians who flourished upon the proceeds of this particular crime. I instructed the police under my control to investigate in certain quarters and effect the necessary arrests.

No result followed.

On further investigation I found that they themselves were in league with the criminals and growing rich on the partnership.

I then proceeded through private sources to gain information and endeavour to effect arrests. Here again I was baulked, for I discovered that an organized terrorism was being exercised towards every one who gave me information. Naturally my information could only be gained from persons more or less connected with that particular social grade; so no sooner was a person seen going to my office, than he was arrested some days later on charges true or false.

Here was a pretty pass! Crime rampant; every source of reaching it closed; the very forces of the State assisting it! I appealed to the Chief of Police, but could gain no credence, or support—scarcely a hearing—in that direction. All I effected was to get his back up for impugning the character of his men.

Here was a position which meant either I must win hands down by proving all I had said, or resign.

I set to work putting my back into it. There

now remained for me only one thing to do. I must go for these police and work up a case strong enough to secure a conviction in a Court of Law and at the same time work up the case against the "pimp" gang in such a way that they and the police could be arrested simultaneously, lest one should take warning by the arrest of the other and find means to circumvent me. Moreover, I had found that it would only be possible fully to tap my sources of information when both were in durance vile.

I worked night and day. In my own person I combined the offices of detective, clerk, Justice of the Peace, policeman et hoc genus omne. I durst trust nobody, for I was surrounded by enemies and spies. One man only I was able to use—Skirving, an old school mate of mine, who is in the service with us. And he helped me like a brick.

Many nights I went to bed wearied out, feeling inclined to give up the struggle and accept defeat; but in the morning determination returned.

To make a long story short, there occurred a split in the ranks of the enemy. Of this I made such use that within a month of the day I started on the job I had packed the Head-centre of the New York pimps in gaol, whilst all the "special" police were removed from special duty, and three of their number were under arrest on criminal charges.

The business did not stop here. The Lieutenant whom I had attacked had the support of the Synod and the Y.M.C.A., he being a zealous member of the Wesleyan Church and his wife of the Dutch. Both the Synod and Y.M.C.A. sent a deputation to remonstrate with me. The officers of the Police Force sent a deputation to the Government asking for my suspension and for an enquiry. The pimps employed the more forcible and primitive argument of "shewtin' irons."

To all these arguments, as well as those supplied by anonymous blackmailing letters, I turned a deaf ear, and went straight through. The case was removed to Pretoria for trial, Johannesburg juries composed of the poorest class of town burghers—no Uitlander being eligible to sit on a jury—rendering the chances of a verdict, where the accused possesses the infamous wealth of those now in the dock, too problematical. Rather I may say, making acquittal certain.

Ex Chief Justice Kotze defended them before the High Court, and after a five days' trial I obtained a verdict convicting them.

Within a short time I shall have a body of special men of my own selection placed at my disposal, for the revelations of the trial have fully justified my action; and then I hope to tackle a few more gangs. What my luck will be I cannot say; but this I know, they have now come to regard me as a factor to be reckoned with, and not merely as " that Quixotic

F. R. M. C. with his cleansing of the Augean stable."

There are many other great abuses still prevailing which our department will have to tackle. This job of mine, cancerous as it was, was but one of the minor evils. If we succeed we shall reap for ourselves the just esteem of every section of the population. If we fail we shall have the consolation of knowing that we have done our best. The job we have undertaken has knocked out more than one man before us; though nobody, hitherto, had tackled it with such a will, or with such a well organized force.

May 21*st.* Behold Ancient Warhorse so far I had got and then I had to stop for want of time!

Since last I was writing Mother has shown me a letter she had from you. It is indeed pleasant to me to hear how happy you are in your distant home. My only regret is, that I cannot sometimes see you and join you in your placid retreat. At times I, too, feel as if I should like to give up all this hurry and bustle, the dust and sweat of the strife and pass my time in peaceful seclusion.

Surely, surely, slumber is more sweet than toil; the shore
Than labour in the deep mid-ocean, wind and wave and oar!
Oh! rest ye, brother Mariners, we will not wander more.

That is my sighing when I go to bed at night tired out, with all my plans seemingly foiled and all my efforts stultified. When it seems to me as I look up against a mountain of injustice and evil that even if One rose from the dead to right it His efforts would be all in vain!

But in the morning after the cold spray I feel

How can man die better than facing fearful odds
For the ashes of his Fathers and the Temples of his Gods.

I mind me, too, of what you once told me, how that all true and honest effort, though seemingly in vain, is not lost energy in the sum total of the Universe.

There is in the grand old traditions of the Old Religion a deal of comforting reflexion. One grows sick of the unlovely cynicism of crude Materialism, with all its selfish inhumanity, next only in degree to the blatant vulgarity of Hell-fire Nonconformity. There are times when one gets in under the teeth of the harrow, and they prick exceeding sore. At such times it is more comforting to contemplate the sublimity of the Kölnischer Dom, or the placid serenity of Socrates' death, than the million dollar profits of all the time-saving machinery in the world.

I am not preaching at you, ou kerel, only the wind is in the wrong quarter to-day.

Do you know where I first heard those lines from Tennyson which I have just quoted? It was nineteen years ago, at Kaffirfontein. You were reading them to us after supper, and I lay on the floor before the fire. What a long, long time ago it seems. You were a comparatively young man then, and I a little "kaalvoet Hotnot." Out in the country the other day I met just such a one, riding a bareback horse. It reminded me of the old days and I felt I should like to change over with him.

When I think, however, of all that has happened since that time, and of what has been achieved by others in the plain pursuit of duty, I am encouraged. "Alles zal regt kom," even if the spikes do prick a bit. "Wat zeg Jakhals? Broer Wolf! slaat yster klauw in de grond?"

> Ride on! the prize is near!
> So pass I hostel, hall, and grange,
> By bridge and ford, by park and pale,
> All armed I ride, whate'er betide,
> Until I find the Holy Grail.

Fate gets up sometimes and hits one an awful crack on the head, when least it is expected, smashes up your cherished ideals, and sets you down, right-about-face, pointing in a brand new direction. Then you've got to grin and say, how nice it is. It helps one to do this when there is an old Joker, out in California, showing one the way how and also where to find the Holy Grail. The gentle breeze from your calm retreat comes to give one courage to look beyond the present troubles, and wait patiently for the healing hand of time.

At such times I more than ever regret that we are separated from each other by half the earth's girdle, and that the period of our acquaintance and association was so brief.

To return to our everyday news.

Last week there was a bit of a scare on, through some arrests which were made of so-called Revolutionists. It is, however, a fiasco; merely a bit of a job worked up by a detective who wanted to gain some kudos. The persons arrested were all indigent loafers, who called themselves captains, etc. The present state of political unrest naturally gave colour to the idea of a revolutionary plot, which greatly favoured the enterprising detective, and there will, of course, have to be a preliminary examination held in the case, but nothing serious can come of it, even though the case goes to trial.

We have in the department just now a great game on hand. The Raad will be asked to place the control of the police and detectives under the State Attorney. This achieved, we shall have some most glorious work before us, extirminating the illicit sale of liquor to natives. We shall also tackle the I. G. B. (illicit gold buying). Both of these evils have assumed such gigantic proportions as to be a menace to the life of the State.

From what I have told you in an earlier part of this letter about another department of crime, you will understand what I mean when I say we are keen about getting the control of the police.

How ramified and how magnificently organized the drink traffic is you will understand when I tell you that it is criminal (punishable as a felony) to give or sell a drop of brandy to a native under any conditions. *Nevertheless*, every Sunday there are fifty thousand Kafirs dead drunk on the reef, and every bottle sold represents a clear profit of four shillings.

The traffic is carried on by huge syndicates of low Jews with vast capital. They possess splendid organizations of large bodies of men, horses, carts, scouts, bruisers, subterranean passages, trap doors, double walls, dummies (to go to prison), and tremendous sinking funds for bribes and rewards. Their emissaries are all over the place. In the lobbies of the Raad, in the halls of the Courts, in the streets, in the clubs, and on 'Change.

They oppose, or support elections, even putting their spoke in the Presidential Election wheel. The whole community groans under them. The clergy denounce them from the pulpit, the State is waterlogged by the burden of their iniquity. They meanwhile grow rich, smoke half-crown cigars, and defy God and man.

The utter eradication, or the overwhelming increase of this evil are the two consequences of our obtaining, or not, the control of the police. All the efforts of our department are, for the moment, bent upon that one object. If we get it, then you'll see the broom go in, even

War Clouds 29

if we get shot for our pains. We have been promised this reward!

This is a glorious field of action. We are just now, with our department of young men, fighting the Armageddon of our country. With us lies the power to do more good, or more evil, than any other in the State; and we are trying our level best to do what we can. At such times it is that the blood tingles, and one does not want just yet to retire into seclusion.

If we can succeed in strangling this one monster of abuse alone, we shall have done much to avert the finger of scorn which is now so readily pointed at us from without. It will also entail a departmental purification, involving nearly one-third of all there unhappily is of corruption at this present moment.

You see the task before us! The shareholders in the Nelmapius Distillery hold very high positions.

June 11th.—Again I am adding a bit to my letter. Since last writing things have got to be rather bad with us in the political world. The Government of this State and the Imperial Government have been haggling for a long time about various points. Just lately the Imperial Government began to push the Franchise question.

Things got a bit ticklish and a conference was arranged between the President and Sir Alfred Milner at Bloemfontein. All this time the malcontent Uitlanders have been kicking up particular fits, and yelling enough to lift the roof off; I may add they have nearly succeeded in doing so.

The conference took place last week. It is needless for me to give you details about it, for we are sending you a paper. Anyway, things have now come to such a pass that unless the policy of this country is conducted with great skill and discretion, we may drift into hostilities with England.

For years past the most violent Jingoes here have assiduously fermented the war spirit in the English people, till they are on the point of forgetting their ancient lofty traditions of fairness. I do not wish to assert that *we* are wholly in the right and have not many grievous errors to make up for. But I *do* contend that Great Britain is at this moment trying to right them by forcing upon us a war of annihilation.

The motives for this seem to me:

(1) Rhodes's covert design to collar the gold mines and rehabilitate the Chartered Company.

(2) Chamberlain's unbounded ambition to extend the Empire.

(3) The fanaticism of those Englishmen who are longing to get square on Majuba and Doornkop, regardless of the justice of the cause in which the Boer on both these occasions fought.

On our side there is the injustice of totally excluding from any voice in public affairs the great portion of the population that bears almost exclusively the cost of administration.

It is impossible to go into all these things here, but the time is critical. Long before you get this letter it will have been decided one way or the other. If we fight, we fight for our existence as a nation. Not only that, it will be the Salamis of the Afrikander race. If it comes we are determined to stand up like men.

If you wish to find me during that period look among the ranks of the people, who for eighty years battled for freedom against as mighty an Empire as the British—and won. If it comes now they will stand with their backs against the rock in their last struggle for final independence or final subjugation. Pray God it may not come!

I have I see indited you much matter, but have told you very little news. News, however, would be difficult to find, for things of daily life are of little interest unless one is a regular correspondent, and able to give them from time to time as they occur, amid the setting of concurrent circumstances. From all I have said, however, you will be able to formulate some idea of our mode of life. Mother and I live together. My house is small but comfortable, and we are in a position to entertain an old friend from the Free State now and again.

With the fixed salary I draw I am relieved from the great worry of considering where next month's supplies are coming from, though my pay is not enough to lay by upon. I keep a pony and trap and four dogs. My work supplies me with vigorous employment and is, in fact, my only strong interest in life. My work, indeed, is my salvation; for without it I should be unfit to fill up space upon the surface of Mother Earth.

I am regarded as happy and successful, and have good prospects before me in life. But for some years past I have felt more and more growing upon me a sense of utter disinterest in all things comprising the sum total of existence.

Naturally one always retains the primitive instinct of self-preservation, but beyond that there is a sense of utter indifference. The only time I really consciously enjoy life is when deeply engaged in the discharge of intricate professional duties, or when taking physical recreation. If I could be a loafer and derive pleasure from it I would loaf. But I cannot. For so many years I have worked continually, that now inactivity tires me. Conviviality and the midnight symposium likewise have no charms for me. I think, if I got into the "tronk" and had to use pick and shovel for eight hours a day, I might succeed in developing a sound interest in my surroundings.

This, my dear Uncle, is a confession I would make to very few, nor is there any good in making it even to you; but we have been good friends so long that I take the privilege of easing myself a bit of that eternal "hump" which gets on my back and rides me for months at a spell.

I am sending you by this mail a photo of myself in three different sittings, as you will then gain a clearer idea of what I look like. It was taken for Mother's birthday.

I hope, now that I have discharged my obligation of writing to you, that you will speedily set your own typewriter in motion. Give my love to Aunt Mary and Cousin Adelaide. Tell the latter not to slay me utterly and put me down for a perfidious liar for not fulfilling my promise to write to her regularly. I mind me that when last I wrote my dog Jim was a little pup with pretty ways; and now, as I write, he sits beside me, a great, vulgar brute, with half his ears chawed off, and bits of other dogs and of coat tails sticking in his teeth.

With hearty greeting to yourself, believe me, my dear Uncle,

Ever your affectionate nephew,
F. R. MOSTYN CLEAVER.

CHAPTER II
AT THE FRONT—IN CRONJE'S LAAGER

(Written in Pencil)

General Cronje's Hoofd Laager,
Modderriver (Magersfontein),
Via Jacobsdal,
Dec. 24th, 1899.

My dearest Mother,

ET me wish you a very happy Xmas. I fear, however, your Xmas will not be so happy as I could wish it, because you will be worrying for my safety. Do not, however, unnecessarily alarm yourself. We are here in a snug corner on the banks of Modderriver. We got here yesterday (Saturday) at the laager, having ridden from Bloemfontein, a three days' journey.

It is quite impossible to imagine, or realize, that one is at the seat of war. The camps are dotted in groups of tents down the river for the space of ten miles. We heave up at a group of tents.

A few men stand about in shirt sleeves smoking and we greet them with: "Dag Kerels!"

At the Front—In Cronje's Laager

"Ja dag!"

"Maak julle oorlog?" (Are you making war?)

"Ja ons pas Laager op!" (Yes, we are minding the camp.)

"Waar's die Engelse?" (Where's the English?)

"D-a-a-a-r Ve-r-r Vijf uur te paard weg!" (*There, far,* five hours on horseback away.)

"Waar's die ander kerels?" (Where's the other fellows?)

"Hulle leg in de schanzes." (Lying in the trenches.)

"Waar?"

"Drie uur te paard hier van daan." (Three hours on horseback from here.)

Now that is my ideal method of going to war. The laager is a rustic assemblage of wagons and tents, about twenty miles beyond the range of the enemy's biggest cannon, where we sit and smoke and play concertina all day long.

About twelve or fifteen miles away in the randtjes sit the men, known as the paarde Commando, who do the fighting. In the laager we are as safe as in Johannesburg, with no worry to keep us awake at night.

I am duly installed under a Veldcornet, and to-night will take my spell of brandwacht (sentry) by sitting behind the wagons smoking. It is, however, merely a formality, as the enemy, before he can reach us, must traverse ten miles of open country, then break through fifteen miles of armed Burghers, and then traverse another twelve miles of open country. Under such circumstances I feel greatly stimulated by the overpowering sense of immediate danger.

Natie (Advocate Ferreira), young Advocate Jorrissen, Judge Esser, and many other acquaintances are here in camp, and looking well and hearty. I have not seen Oom Naas (Commandant General Ferreira), and do not expect to as he is now a General, having been appointed in place of General Prinsloo, who resigned after Rooilaagte.

I have not yet met any of the Ladybrand fellows. They, too, are away out in the trenches.

It is traditionally hot and dry out here. On these flats there has not been a drop of rain for months. In the middle of the day we lie under the wagons and "gaap zoo's kraaie" (gape like crows).

Everything is still in the fighting line. The enemy are "schuw" (shy) since the last battle (the slaughter of the Scots at Magersfontein). There is no further attack expected for some time to come. When it arrives, it will find our people still more strongly fortified than before.

All the newspaper reports are inadequate to convey a full idea of the severity of the reception accorded the enemy in the last battle. They have not even yet interred all their men who fell. In our camp there is no single word of boasting; but one hears constant expressions of sympathy for the poor soldiers who have been sacrificed to the ambition of politicians.

There is, however, a stern determination to stand firm. The Free Staters have been fighting like lions to wipe out the stain of their previous defeats.

There is nothing more to tell you, life is so peaceful and quiet in camp. I am in the best of health and spirits.

With very best love, believe me, my dear Mother, truly and affectionately your son,

REG.

> General Cronje's Hoofd Laager,
> Modderriver,
> Dec. 31st, 1899.

My dear Mother,

Let me wish you a very happy New Year. We do not get much opportunity to write, so I am availing myself of Oom Naas's camp table in his tent. I came over here last evening to pay him a visit, and am leaving again presently for my own laager, where I have made myself a schuilplek inside a big bush out in the veld, far away from the reach of bombs, where I lie on my back and sleep, and, if necessary, ride a message for the General.

There has been no fighting since I came to these parts, though the cannon from the opposing camps take occasional pot shots at each other. Nobody is ever hurt by them, and we are only aware of the fact by the distant boom which reaches us. Some time ago, at night, there was a false alarm in the schanzes, and our people kept up a hot fire at nothing for about fifteen minutes. We in the laager, twelve miles away, heard it, and turned out with our guns into the kopje, where we stood guard from 8 p.m. till 2.30 a.m. This is the closest I have been to active service. If I go on standing fire at that rate I shall grow quite brave!

Two of our horses got stolen last Sunday almost from under our very noses, and have not since been seen. The result is that two of the four of us are placed hors de combat, and are degraded to the rank of laager wacht. We had a nice fall of rain this week, which has made the air much cooler. Further, nothing of note has occurred, and the English do not look like attacking. I surmise they intend to sit still, for the purpose of cutting us off from the Colony.

The man is just waiting to take away the post, so I must close. Oom Naas sends greeting. He is here with Pieter, Stefanus, Cornelis (his sons), Hans Koppies, Blaauw, Jan Taal, Hannis van Reenen, and others of your old boys. I am in excellent health and spirits.

With very best love, I am, my dear Mother,
Truly and affectionately your son,
REG.

On 7 January the Chief Detective handed me a telegram: Modderriver, Cleaver. Cleaver per Hoofd Speurder. Ben nog frisch en gezond geen gelegenheid tot schrijven. (Am still well and hearty. No opportunity to write.)

At the Front—In Cronje's Laager

But a few days later came the following, dated c/o Hoofd Commandant Ferreira.

Scholznek,
Jan. 14th, 1900.

My dear Mother,

It is now a fortnight since last I wrote, though last Saturday I sent you a wire, saying I was well. Such is about the full extent to which one's literary efforts attain under the prevailing conditions. I get up in the morning and roll up my blanket, with a vague impression that I must "van daag skrijve." The impression lasts several days, when it shapes itself into action.

But in looking for writing material I remember that I have used my writing paper for wrapping up "stormjagers" (cakes fried in fat), and that owing to grease it will no longer retain the impression of ink; while my pen I have utilized for pinning up a bucksail.

On application to Hans Koppies for "skrijvgoed," he replies: "J-a-a! Blauw het laaste die pen gehad, om papte roer." "Nee!" says Blauw, " Piet het hom nog na die gebruik, om de paerd zy poot uit te krap, en de enkpotje het Jannie achter de volstruis stukkent gekooi!" (Well Blauw was the last who had the pen, to stir the porridge. Nay, says Blauw, Piet used him after that to scrape out the horse's hoof, and Johnny broke the inkpot, throwing it after the ostrich.)

So it goes on, and when finally the materials are got together, writing is almost impossible. I am now sitting under a tree, holding down the paper with stones and laboriously forming each letter.

So far I have only received from you one letter—the one you enclosed to "Oom Naas" (the Commandant). I trust you are no longer worrying so badly about my safety. Because one is at the seat of war, one's not necessarily in danger of getting shot. I, too, at first imagined that when one approached within twenty miles of the laager the zone of danger began. But I now find that the laager is about as dangerous as a nachtmaal gathering (Sacrament Service). Even the schanzes themselves, twelve miles distant from the nearest laager, are quite safe, except when a battle is in progress—at which time the death rate is very little higher than that of Bloemfontein in the hot season.

Since I came to these parts the English have fired at our schanzes about two hundred to three hundred bombs, and have only succeeded in wounding seven men. The majority of our casualties lately have arisen through our men boring with gimlets and red hot irons into unexploded English Lyddite bombs in order to ascertain the contents.

There has been no fighting at all, nor do we anticipate any for some time. That report in the paper about Commandant Ferreira having gone out with a patrol and getting three of his men wounded by shells was an incorrect jumble sent up by a fatheaded reporter twenty-five miles from the scene of events. The true

At the Front—In Cronje's Laager

account is that some of Oom Naas' men and others under another leader went out on a patrol and came back sleek and full of "lekker varsche vleesch en konfyt" (nice fresh meat and jam), which friendly farmers treated them to; while on the same day, at another place, twelve miles away, three of the above reported seven were wounded.

If O'Flaherty (of the "Leader") were here, I'd give him a few notes to correct all the bluff he wrote about the Lyddite bomb. Its alleged two hundred yards of desolation is rot. It blows a big hole in the ground about eight feet in diameter, makes a horrible noise, and emits a poisonous gas, and further does no more harm than any other shell of its size.

The lancers he threatened us with are a disappointment likewise. For the foot regiments our burghers have more respect, and speak in the highest terms of their bravery.

I have now been with Oom Naas a fortnight. Nothing of any moment has happened during that time, except that I took the first prize for cooking, when my turn came round. I anticipate, however, that I shall be awarded the gold medal for sleeping soon.

Oom Naas has been elected Hoofd Commandant (Commander-in-Chief) of the Western Frontier, and to-morrow he is moving up to Kimberley or Scholznek—we are not there actually at the Nek, although I have dated from there.

The laager will remain where it is, but I think he will take Cornelis, Stephanus (his sons) and me with him as staff—for Secretaries. Our duty will then be to regulate the campaign, and conduct the administration, without going into any fighting. Oom Naas was very unwilling to accept the promotion and only did so after strong representations from his burghers, by whom he is greatly beloved, and from the Government, who think very highly of him.

At Magersfontein he behaved with distinguished bravery. During the severest fire—a roaring cannonade from forty-two guns—he galloped up across the flats, dismounted and ran forward a few hundred yards, all in the open, followed by the Ladybranders and Kroonstaders, and took up his position on the bare flats at the central point of the main British attack. A stranger, who has fought in three wars, who witnessed this incident as a spectator, told me that your old pupils (the Ladybranders) walked into the very gates of Hades with the nerve and coolness of old soldiers. From themselves I have heard nothing about this bravery. In fact throughout the whole army there is a marked absence of boastfulness, though everybody is filled with determination.

Kimberley is in sore straits. Natives we catch coming out are terribly emaciated, and all tell the same tale of starvation. Horseflesh, they say, has been eaten since January the 8th, and even the poor beasts we capture can scarcely

At the Front—In Cronje's Laager 43

walk. On Jan. 3rd we heard severe firing inside the town and put it down to civil strife. A Hottentot subsequently captured said it was mutiny among the troops—(So *like* a Hottentot's yarn!—Ed.). More recent prisoners report that Rhodes goes about with a bodyguard of forty men to protect him from attacks (!).

I hope Jim, Sambo, and Robin are all well. My original leave expires on Monday, but it is now extended to the end of this month, when I shall return home. I can't say what day I shall be there, but it will be somewhere after February 1st. The weather keeps very dry, but is not so hot as previously.

It is no use your writing any more after receipt of this, but my telegraphic address is c/o Commandant Ferreira, Scholznek. Keep up your spirits and don't be alarmed about me. I am as fit as a fiddle and quite safe.

With very best love, believe me, my dear Mother,

   Truly and affectionately your son,
           REG.

The next letter is dated

     C/o Commandant Ferreira,
      Ladybrand Laager,
       Modderriver,
        Via Jacobsdal,
         24.1.1900.

My dear Mother,

The above is my correct address. Since writing to you some days back I have had two letters from you; one dated January 5th, and one Jan. 11th.

I am not returning at the end of the month, since I have been granted extension of leave until they (my superiors in the department) send for me. Do not harrow yourself by unnecessary alarms, and do not sap my courage by imparting those feelings to me in your letters. The only effect it has upon me, is to drive me a step nearer danger; for the more I become convinced that I am a coward, the more I bring myself to face danger in order to recover my self respect. One thing you may take for certain. I am here doing what I consider to be my duty; and I will rather die of the fright I may entertain than run away and show it.

Your anticipations of the darkest side positively unnerve me. Did I feel perfectly assured of my own courage, I might, without love of self respect, exercise a healthy caution to the fullest degree consistent with duty; but when I do not entertain that feeling, I cannot adopt such a course. If you feel yourself unable to display the firmness required of us all at this time, then rather refrain from writing.

If Thomas (the groom—now general houseboy, which he resented—Ed.) becomes opstandig, let Menton or Sheppard speak to him in such terms as best appeal to his nature (the " cat ").

Oom Naas has left here and gone to Olifantsfontein to take up his duties as Hoofd Commandant—Commandant General of the West.

At the Front—In Cronje's Laager

Christoffel Froneman of Senekal is now Commandant of the Ladybrand Laager in his place. We are doing nothing just now but eating and sleeping.

For the last nine or ten days the English have been furiously bombarding the centre of our line of trenches, occupied by the Transvaalers and a detachment of the O.F.S. and also by our left wing. One day they fired over four hundred shells into the line. On other days the fire has varied from one hundred to three hundred and fifty.

The only damage done by some three thousand shells dropped into our lines during this week has been: three men slightly wounded, one buck wagon and the wheel of one ammunition wagon smashed, one ammunition chest blown up, two or three cattle killed, and one horse. I sometimes climb a hill and watch the operation through a glass.

The enemy has made several feints by marching out in considerable force with both infantry and cavalry. On each occasion our guns have dropped a few shots among them, upon which they have invariably retired. There seems to be no intention on their part to make a general attack.

I do not know when I shall return. Unless I am previously sent for by Louis (Acting State Attorney Jacobsz), I shall stay another six or eight weeks.

Kimberley is to-day very heavily bombarded

by our guns. We are about eighteen miles distant here and can hear the booming from time to time.

Wally Coleman is now here in command of the Bloemfonteinas. He is Veldcornet and has greatly distinguished himself in previous battles. All the old schoolboys send you "greetings."

With my best love to you, believe me, my dearest Mother,

Sincerely and affectionately your son,

REG.

On 30 January I had not received the last two letters. I then wrote to him:

Johannesburg,
30th Jan. 1900.

My dearest Son,

I do so wish you would find time to write to me. Van der Merwe is returning, van Os is back, Ferreira is bombarding Kimberley; but of you or your whereabouts I know nothing. All day long my thoughts are with you and your poor sisters, and as soon as I sleep, war and trouble are in my dreams. I suppose others around me and in all ages have had to suffer so. Mine is only the common lot of women.

The 14th was the last date of your writing. Your last telegram the 26th. You said you were "moving West." What did that mean? I have not seen van Os, but Pieter Fischer tells me, van Os says you do not mean to come back.

I wired on the 27th and also posted a letter. It seems you never get my letters. I have written *many*.

Sheppard is now occupying Dr. Davies's house as a protection to it. Some people were put into Kendal Franks's and proceeded to sell twelve dozen sheets and other valuables.

The town has been turned upside down for nearly a month over the withdrawal of permits. Now suddenly comes a change. Nobody is to go. Everyone is to get his permit back. I wish some word could come from Lily and Nancy. I am so cut off from you all. People are very kind to me, being sorry for my loneliness.

I see Abram Greyling of Mon Répos is wounded. Poor fellow!

31st.

Yours of 24th was sent over to me by Mr. Menton. I am very sorry you are staying so long away; but I have to grin and bear it—or *not*—as the case may be. I have been trying all day to come across van Os, but vainly. Mr. Vos (of your office) tells me van Os says you are well and enjoying yourself; never still for a moment.

Please don't talk rubbish about your own cowardice. You are perfectly foolhardy. Always were; just as when you climbed those dreadful mountain peaks to get the vulture's eggs.

Give my love to all my boys and to General "Naas." Phil is just playing his banjo. He feels quite cheerful since he has had his permit returned. But he *can't* get his receipts for his commandeered stock, although I have been with him more than once to the office. Brink is commandeered and leaves to-morrow. I have heard nothing more of the two Bothas, who left for Ladysmith.

Of course I know nothing of "Foughten Fields"; but to the *lay* mind there does seem something remarkable, not to say miraculous, in the fact that *three thousand* bombs only succeed in giving slight flesh wounds to two burghers; whilst *every single* Boer bomb slays its thousands!

In reading similar statements in the "Standard and Diggers," from the pen of v. Gelder, I concluded that the fearful havoc had been wrought with Samson's weapon (the jawbone of an ass), but since *you* repeat the same things, they must be true! But how do you account for it? My neighbour, Mrs. Herbert, says she has it from eye-witnesses of the fact, that every time the Boers trek out to fight, two Shining Beings, on White Horses, go before and turn the bombs aside.

Good-bye my son; may God guard you and bring you back to me, whose Light of Life you are.

Your ever loving,
MOTHER.

CHAPTER III
THE PRIESKA EXPEDITION (1900)

N 26 January 1900 the following telegram was handed to me by Chief Detective Menton:

Van Cleaver.
    Aan Cleaver by Hoofd Speurder.
"I am still well and probably leaving here and going further west in a couple of days."

A few days later the same official handed me a letter addressed to his care by my son. It was written in pencil upon what looked like a leaf of an old account book and ran:

                        Scholtznek,
                        Jan. 26, 1900.
My dear Mother,
    I wrote to you a few days ago and now I just drop you a few lines to say I have received your wire and letter and shall be on the lookout for the hamper, though I fear it will be pilfered by transport riders, like some Xmas sweets Oom Naas (Commandant Ignatius Ferreira) recently had sent him.

My chief object in writing was to tell you that I am leaving here to-day along with a little expeditionary force of ours which is being sent west across the Orange River. I am going in the capacity of legal adviser, as such advice will be particularly necessary in connection with proclamations and so forth. I don't know how long we shall remain away; in all probability for a long time. Do not infer my decease if I shall, in future, not have written for some time; for there will be *no post or telegraph* service at the start, and we shall have to send letters by opportunity, when we can get one. The place we are bound for is Prieska. My address remains unchanged, they will forward my post from here.

Our mission is political and not military, for the first while at any rate, as the English are remote from those parts at present.

If you wish to remit me any special message send to Hoofd Commandant Ferreira, Olifantsfontein, Kimberley, and he will know where to send it.

With very best love from me, my dear Mother,
Your affectionate son,
REG.

The moving cause of this expedition, from which the Burgher Government hoped so much, was a deputation sent from Prieska asking that a small force should be sent West, which should take possession of the small

The Prieska Expedition (1900) 51

towns. These being so distant from the seat of war were completely undefended. They should then commandeer the subjects of the Cape Colony in those parts, who would thus, in case of things going wrong, escape the penalties of high treason, as having acted under compulsion. The North-west being thus secured, it would not be difficult to make a descent upon Cape Town, which was more or less left open, the troops being required in the north, where Kimberley was besieged and the whole country in rebellion.

The West and North-west seemed thus an easy prey. Commandant Ferreira, a man of chivalrous honour, feared only one thing—that mischief and inhumanity might be wrought by a troop of rebels against neighbours who might possibly remain loyal to the Queen. One man in his laager he had known from childhood, and knew him to be like-minded with himself.

That man was Advocate Mostyn Cleaver. He was given the military rank of Veldcornet, about equal to that of Major, and attached to the expedition. "I want you most of all, Reggy," he said, "to see that no outrages are committed, nothing done contrary to the usages of honourable warfare. That before all. Then see that what we conquer is securely annexed to the Orange Free State. This must be done at once, and the colonists made to swear allegiance to us as they promise by their deputation. It is not only necessary for us but to shield them from the consequences of high treason, while fighting under our flag, which you must at once commandeer them to do."

Three weeks later than the previous letter the following came to hand:

>Griquastad,
>Feb. 10th, 1900.

My dear Mother,

We are in a town for a few hours and a post of some sort will probably be despatched some time or other, from here to somewhere else, consequently I take the opportunity of writing to let you know how I am. My health is excellent and my appetite Herculean. My clothes are such that, compared to me, Phil (a friend who scorned appearances—Ed.) is spruce and neat. My hair and beard, which to-day I have for the first time through many weeks seen reflected in a mirror, are positively shaggy. (N.B.—Formerly he was very neat and somewhat of a dandy—Ed.)

On the whole I was never in better condition at any time I can remember. We have been camping along the Modder and Vaal Rivers, so that we have had a chance to keep clean, although in camp we had sometimes to be content with a bath once in eight days. (At home, ill or well, he must have his morning tub, if the heavens fell—Ed.)

Unfortunately I have lost one of my horses, that stout pony I used to drive in Johannesburg.

He got some mysterious illness through being unused to the country, and had to be left behind at Douglas. I have, however, still one horse left, which Oom Stoffel Froneman gave me when I left Magersfontein.

Commandant Steenekamp, the one who led the rear attack at Stormberg, has joined us as Hoofd Commandant of our expedition. He is a very able man and inspires great confidence. He has attached me to his person as legal adviser to our undertaking.

Of our undertaking and our future movements I am not entitled to write, so I cannot say where I shall be next; but you will doubtless see from the papers all we do and where we have gone.

There has been no fighting along this border, except that an affair of outposts—so we hear by despatch riders—took place at Koodoosberg, some forty miles from here, between a regiment of English troops and some burghers from Magersfontein.

The land—the wilderness of thorns—still continues. At times we have gone a couple or three hours at a stretch where it was impossible to turn twenty yards out of the road for thorn bushes.

The heat, which is very great, we are now quite accustomed to, and find it invigorating and not in any way relaxing, like that of Pretoria or Natal.

Since leaving Bloemfontein I have only *once*

slept under a roof, and now I quite prefer sleeping in the open.

I shouldn't mind just now having a couple of the oldest of my discarded coats and waistcoats—do not send them, for they would never reach me. They would pass muster in laager as swell toff outfits and would fetch heaps of tobacco and oxriems—the camp medium of exchange—at a public auction! The boots and trousers I brought with me were good quality and last well. The chief consumption is in hats; for I invariably sleep in mine, and also use it for a cushion when sitting upon thorny parts of the veld. I have re-acquired all my old veld craft, and know the exact turn to which to bake a stormjager or aschkoek. I have also greatly overcome my aversion to raw meat and can cut up a beast fairly well.

I received a letter from you, which was forwarded to me on the road hither. My functions here are purely pacific. The Commandant does not take me with him on patrol, but leaves me in charge of his papers. I was very sorry to disappoint you by not returning home when you expected me; but I felt it my duty to accept the commission of legal adviser when offered me, and thereby discharge an important office in what may prove to be the most weighty place in the development of our Great National Struggle. More especially as there was nobody else at hand who possessed the necessary qualifications.

The Prieska Expedition (1900)

My functions pertain purely to the shaping of law and order, and to the mitigation of the lawlessness inevitably attendant upon war. Is my Mother reassured?

Remember me to friends. Say I have not written because it is all I can do to get written a letter to you now and again.

How are Robin and Jim and Sambo? God bless you, my dear Mother, and believe me truly your son,

REG.

The next missive handed me by the Hoofd Speurder (Chief Detective) was enclosed in an envelope across which was printed "On Her Majesty's Service." This legend was broadly struck through by a pen, and underneath stood in my son's handwriting " In dienst O. V. Staat op commando." It did not reach Johannesburg until the 11th of March, having been three weeks and a day on the road. It was dated:

Prieska,
17—2—1900.

My dearest Mother,

I am still well and hearty but dreadfully busy.

Report rider leaves at once. His horse is saddled already.

Love,
REG.

This was written on a scrap of waste paper, on the reverse side of which stood in pencil:

Kieze door burgers van geproclameerd dis-

trikt, van verschillende hoofden 5 leden. . . .
Als candidaten staan de volgende heeren.

(Election by burghers of the proclaimed district of different Officials. Five Members [the next word illegible]. The following gentlemen stand as Candidates.)

So this morsel of waste paper told us that the northern districts were already proclaimed Free State territory and annexed! and civil Government was being inaugurated.

Yet the burghers were scandalized when *their* territory, after being fought for and conquered step by step, was annexed!

A day or two later came the following:

Prieska,
Feb. 21st 1900.

My dearest Mother,

Doubtless by now you will be glad to get a letter from me, after my long silence. I have from time to time been able to post you just a word to state that I am alive and well, though I cannot say if these letters ever reached you. There is no regular post and we have to rely on occasional despatch riders who may be traversing any portion of the homeward road. Sometimes we have only five minutes' notice of his departure. This letter I shall myself take through as far as our little laager on the banks of the Orange River, six hours from here, as I am going up there to consult with the General to-night.

The Prieska Expedition (1900) 57

This has been one of the most dashing bits of work during the war. So far we have not fired a shot; but the enterprise, daring, and promptitude displayed by our little band and by their leaders have been most praiseworthy.

We left Griquastad—whence I wrote you a long letter—on a Saturday evening, and travelled over some very heavy roads on Sunday and Monday. On Monday evening we inspanned at sunset on the edge of a broad strip of Dorstland (waterless land) north of the river. It was no use outspanning, for there was neither grass nor water, except at one point, where there was a well. We pushed on steadily till nearly midnight through a long mountain pass, and then outspanned, tied up our horses to bushes, and lay down to sleep. Before we had closed our eyes a report came that the enemy was approaching the pont from the opposite bank to seize the crossing.

Instantly we mounted again and pushed on through heavy sand and hard gravel alternately as fast as our poor flagging beasts could carry us. It was a strange sight to see, and still stranger to experience, that little party of men resolutely clattering on through the moonlight! Men and beasts fagged to the uttermost, but not a word of complaint. Some chatting, some singing, some solemnly smoking; each one from time to time looking to the slot of his rifle.

We reached the river at 3 a.m. and drew our horses under cover, when man and beast just lay down together on the sand. We were only about thirty-five in number. The Chiefs held consultation on the edge of the water.

The pont was down and the river deep, broad, and swift. The Commandant and four men stripped, laid the guns on a small raft, and plunged in to swim across, pushing the raft with them.

At dawn they landed on the other side, scaled the banks and surrounded the house of the pont-keepers, whom they took prisoners.

The next to cross was a party of four, including myself, who escorted the Commander-in-Chief across.

We then swam some horses and men over and sent out a patrol. From that moment for the next two and a half days we lived like naked savages in the water, working like Trojans and with no appliances save our hands and a large degree of Boere-plane to restore the pont. And we did it! By the time our main body and wagons arrived the pont was working.

At sunset the third day we again saddled up and rode slap through the night, with an advance guard, quite small in number, to Prieska. I have done several heavy marches, but this was the heaviest I ever experienced. Men literally slept on their horses' backs. Towards morning we were bound to rest an hour to prevent the men dropping in the road.

At dawn our Commandant rode into the town with six men and took possession of the Land-

The Prieska Expedition (1900)

drost's Office and of the Gaol and Post and Telegraph Offices, and closed the canteens.

At 8.30 we rode in and hoisted the flag and read the proclamation. The Resident Magistrate and all public officials received their passports and are gone, and we are busy doing the work for which we came here.

I have been sitting as Magistrate and have been busy night and day organizing the new order of things. I am not at liberty to tell you what we are doing, or going to do, or anything else about the undertaking; for this letter might not reach you.

We are almost entirely without news for the last fortnight or more. There has been heavy fighting at Magersfontein and Kimberley. We could hear the firing about one hundred and twenty miles away, but we do not know the result, though we understand the troops have pushed forward considerably.

I fear you have been greatly alarmed on my account, but I had no means of letting you know of my safety, and I relied on your having been already in receipt of my letters stating that I was leaving Magersfontein.

I am glad I came with this expedition. The amount of good work I have been able to do for the cause is far greater than I ever anticipated. Our work may yet be crowned by being the final and immediate cause of a United Free Flag throughout South Africa. I hold this, even should the worst have happened at Magersfontein.

You would hardly know me now, tanned, bearded, and as hale and hearty as a brick. My duties now are entirely in a different sphere, as they are making use of my head and not of my rifle. Of course I have not heard from you, or anybody, since I left Douglas, though doubtless many letters await me in the laager.

I see they have fought again desperately in Natal and Colesberg.

I don't know when I shall return home again. Probably, nay almost certainly, not before the war is over. I long for home sometimes, but here is my duty. It is proved to me more conclusively every day, and I do that duty with ardour. My thoughts are often with you, and I am confident in the hope that we shall live to see each other again. Remember me to Robin, Jim, and Sambo. (Horse and dogs—Ed.) With best love to yourself, believe me, my dearest Mother,

Your most affectionate son,

REG.

Whilst he was indulging such bright hopes for the future, his generosity had opened wide the door for the speedy extinction of them all in giving safe conduct and freedom to the officials, instead of keeping them prisoners of war as the burghers desired. He argued, that as they were civilians and non-combatants it would be ungenerous to detain them.

A few miles from the village the officials met the Post Cart on its weekly and bi-weekly

The Prieska Expedition (1900) 61

journey towards the north. This they naturally turned back, and at the earliest opportunity, on reaching the nearest telegraph station, wired news to Cape Town.

The surprise, perhaps even consternation, it caused there must have been considerable. The authorities do not seem to have imagined the Boers would venture upon such an expedition with so inconsiderable a force as three hundred men.

They heard, too, that the expedition was led by an English gentleman, a man of considerable powers of organization and resource, gifted, moreover, with a golden tongue, which he was using to some purpose in both languages in persuading the people to join in the great movement for a United Republican South Africa.

Of course they made some mistakes. In the light that the origin of the expedition was a deputation from the northern districts, inviting the co-operation of the Orange Free State burghers in a contemplated rising, my son's speech to them was as much a part of their programme as was the *commandeering* for military service.

Another mistake of Kitchener's was in thinking that Mostyn Cleaver was a British subject. He was born and bred in the Orange Free State, to which he was passionately attached. Until adolescence he had been very little in contact with individual English except myself. Then came his four years' study at home. He was also an admitted burgher of the Transvaal and an official. So that on every side his allegiance was due to the Republics.

He loved and looked up to England as the model upon which he desired the Republics to be formed, not a little also because it was his mother's deeply beloved native land. But much as he deprecated the war and strove to avert it, yet once it began he never hesitated as to the part duty and honour demanded of him. "England is your land, Mother, and you are right to love and abide by it; but Africa is mine. Had I a thousand lives I would give them all for my country."

But Lord Kitchener set out for the north, breathing vengeance against the "renegade Englishman"; and Sir Alfred Milner would not have spared him a traitor's doom had he escaped a bullet on the field and been taken prisoner.

Meantime I, blind mortal! was hoping and praying he might be taken prisoner; firstly to save his dear life, and secondly that he might not have the blood of any countryman of mine on his hands.

Things in other quarters were changing. The tide of disaster had turned from the British and was sweeping back on the Boers. Before I got my son's next letter Kimberley was relieved, Cronje's army had surrendered, Ladysmith was relieved, the besieging armies put to flight, and Bloemfontein was taken.

A great blow for us both was the death of

Commandant General Ferreira, beloved as a brother by myself and as a father by my son. As soon as I heard of the misadventure I went to the authorities of Johannesburg for a passport to go down and nurse him. But they told me he had fallen dead on the spot where he received the fatal bullet.

The next letter from my son that reached Johannesburg was addressed to his successor in the Veldcornetcy of the Rust en Orde:

Prieska, Orange Free State,
Feb. 25th, 1900.

My dear . . .,

Verily and of a sooth I am accursed by thee. Else why those qualms of conscience whereby I have been afflicted these eight weeks past? Many a time and oft I have felt that I ought to write to you, and have even got so far as to begin but no farther. You know what it is like out in camp. One's literary talents don't scintillate when one has to lie under the wagon in a yard of dust with tar dropping from above. One uses the sole of a sleeping neighbour's boot for a writing pad, since the soap-bowl he was just now using has been claimed by the vleesch-corporal, "om stormjagers op te maken." The pen does not fit deftly to the finger of the scribe, since that yesterday Gert used it to spit a zout-ribbetje upon and but half a minute since the scribe himself stirred his coffee with it, omitting afterwards to wipe it clean upon his trousers. The paper is oily from having been packed in the same saddle-bag with hot carbonatjes, and the ink is scarce because that plague of the laager, the tame ostrich, recently prowling, picked up and tried to swallow the pot, spilling half of the contents into his gullet!

Grand life this is! Healthy, irresponsible. At times utter indolence and at times grim hard work to the utmost limits of human endurance. The constant presence of danger and familiarity with sudden death, which one anticipates as one's own probable portion at any moment of the day or night, have entirely lost their terrors and only seem to operate as an extra quickening stimulus to add zest to life. I have often heard and read of that peculiar characteristic as being the result of campaigning, though I could never understand the possibility of it in good earnest till experiencing it in my own person.

This campaign has been a great experience. I started it in good earnest, taking my full share in every duty which devolves upon the burgher, even down to the cooking and cutting up of oxen. At the start I was drafted into the Lancers, a body of six hundred mounted reserves, picked men who lay in the bush behind the main positions at Magersfontein, with their horses ready night and day to do all patrol work and reinforcement wherever necessary.

After about ten days of this work, which I liked very much, I got leave to join the Lady-

The Prieska Expedition (1900)

brand Commando under Hoofd Commandant Ferreira. The work here was different. We spent the days behind the kopje in camp, and at night we went round to the front of the kopje and lay in the trenches.

In course of time it came to pass that I was made Rechtsgeleerdte Adviseur to the Krijgsraad van den Rechtervleugel (legal adviser to the Council of War of the right wing—Ed.) I was also every fourth day cook to the Commandant's mess.

Despite these lofty honours I continued to occupy my trench and take my turn at guard at night. I was told I might leave them off, but I preferred it as being a pleasant variety. Fortunately I never slept on guard, but had I done so there might have arisen a fatal conflict of positions. Thus the Publiek Aanklager van den Krijgsraad, prosecuting the sleeping burgher for plichtsverzuim (neglect of duty), the burgher defending himself and accusing the Publiek Aanklager (Public Prosecutor) of vindictiveness, while the cook demanded freedom from attendance on the Krijgsraad in order to attend to zoutribetjes (ribs of salted meat).

I remained at Magersfontein until about January 28th. Many things happened there, but at this remote period of time it is quite impossible to relate them. I went on many patrols and was frequently awakened at early dawn by the shells exploding in our trenches. We'd jump up and dive into our schanzes like a drove of meercats, thinking on each occasion that "now we were in for it." But all the time I was there I never fired a shot.

I hear there have been some extensive operations since I left, but as yet we have no detailed information. We have heard nothing since we crossed the pale into this wilderness three weeks ago.

We get hold of English reports which tell us of the total annihilation of the Western Boer forces (true enough, notwithstanding their unbelief—Cronje's surrender—Ed.), and many more things besides; but it is impossible to believe them, for these reports, which we found here, concerning Spion's Kop and other brilliant Boer victories [sic] represented the Boers as being thrashed out of all recognition.

That there has been heavy fighting we know, for on the 15th and previous days, when we crossed the Orange River at a point 22 or 23 hours from Kimberley, we distinctly heard the big guns booming.

You have doubtless long ago writ me down a trifler with truth. I told you when I left that I was not going to do a "guy" upon my friends in Johannesburg, and such was then my honest intention. But when my month was up, it seemed so pitifully short, that I asked for an extension, which was granted me up to the end of January, and, subsequently, without my asking for it, was made onbeperkt (unlimited).

Just then this expedition to Prieska and the

The Prieska Expedition (1900)

Western Provinces was started. The force sent was small, ludicrously small, for the gigantic work of trekking right away into the desert, beyond the range of communication or reinforcement, and going to set the remaining portions of Africa in a blaze.

The enterprise was attended with the greatest possible danger, not only to the individuals of which it was composed, but also to the cause, if it should fail; while on the other hand its success would probably insure the ultimate success of the war.

There was no legal adviser accompanying it, and so it was resolved to send me after the main party to fulfil that function. I knew that in accepting that office I debarred myself from all possibility of seeing my home again before the war was over, but I also realized that I would be the means, under the circumstances, of doing more for the Cause than a hundred like me could perform under the conditions.

Therefore it was that I came and the issue has proved the correctness of my anticipations. We left Magersfontein about January 28th or 29th and travelled very slowly as far as Douglas, owing to our preparations not being in order. It took us nearly a fortnight to negotiate that bit.

There were two patrols of the enemy hanging on our rear all the time, one of about fifteen hundred men and one of a thousand. They did not, however, attack, and twice when we rode out to meet them they moved out of reach. I don't know why they did not attack us, for they were more than ten to one, had they only known it. We had about two hundred Griquas. The Griquas are like the fifth leg of a calf; they are a curiosity and cost a lot, but ain't no use, except to eat up oxen.

From Douglas we trekked to Griquatown, the Hoofd Commandant and his staff, including myself, going on ahead.

This is a beautiful country all the way from Modder River to here. You may reckon always on not having to go more than forty-five miles to the next water. One fine advantage of this system is that it enables both man and beast to get up a real, solid thirst. I would certainly recommend it to those whose jaded palates no longer permit them to enjoy their drinks. A further stimulus is to be found in the natural brackishness of the water. I usually lick a bit of rock salt in order to restore a taste of freshness after the water.

Should the English happen to have visited the well before us and have wrecked the windlass, we find it necessary to link together ox riems and haul up water in a hat. In such a case we find it best to select a fine, old, seasoned hat, which has done service since the first commando. An article of this description not only possesses the advantage of being watertight, but also imparts a blend to the saltness of the water.

The Prieska Expedition (1900)

Should one at any time feel tired, do not hesitate at once to sit down, without consideration as to where you shall sit; for such consideration would be utterly wasted. One spot is as good as another; they are all equally covered with thorns. Take that as an axiom.

I have heard some men say there is a difference, namely, as to the form and quality of the thorns. Naturally, if a man is particular and has plenty of time to select, let him do so. It may be that he has a special vanity to gratify, or that an especial nerve is stimulated by the knowledge that the thorn, on which he sits, is a dubbeltje, a haak-en-steek, adriedoorn-haak, a wacht-a-beetje, a krap-en-scheur, a duivel's jaap, or a klits-en-klauw. But to me such distinctions are trivial. The time wasted therein might better be occupied some other way—for instance in pulling out the thorns. We have grown quite experts in this. Even as monkeys hunt for fleas at sunrise, sunset, midday and in between, so we pull out the thorns.

The sole theory I can formulate upon the subject is, that somewhere in the remote ages of the past the forest trees elsewhere cast out and banished one of their number because he became diseased and developed thorns. Now this fellow roamed the world, seeking a new place in which to strike root, and finally selected the Kalahari.

The native trees were small and humble, and in their rustic simplicity imagined that this foreign bounder represented the height of civilization and fashion. Through a species of snobbery they copied his vices, until at last they became as depraved as himself, and now, such is the force of public opinion among them, that should there by chance arise a tree without thorns, they instantly wither him with scorn and he hangs his head and dies of shame.

Such ticks, too, of every sort and all varieties as abound! When they catch a grip, it requires brute force to sever the connection. I seriously think of devising a patent consisting of a trained bushtick, which shall grip the thorns imbedded in the human frame, while two men pull him back by the legs. Everything, intelligently directed, has its uses.

Griquatown was the last place where I was conscious of a date, and even then it was a wrong one. We pushed on ruthlessly day and night through sand, stones, bush, and water till one morning at dawn we found ourselves outside Prieska, which we promptly annexed and proclaimed. The Commandant ordered me to write out and affix the proclamation. That was easy enough until I got to the date. I asked him the day of the week and he could not tell. I asked the secretary, the four adjutants, and twenty-five men the same question equally in vain. I appealed to the local inhabitants. The British portion refused to tell, saying they hoped I would affix a wrong date and render the proclamation void, while our partisans thought I was joking. At last I captured a small boy, and by a bribe of sweets I learnt that it was Friday. I was then able by a process of back calculation extending over three weeks to locate the date as Friday, the 16th February, 1900. Fine life this! It gives plenty of scope for mental exercise! So, you see, our only occupation isn't pulling out thorns.

We have done some splendid mobilization. We moved so rapidly, that nobody knew of our presence. When we rode into Prieska we simultaneously entered the bedrooms of the respective officials and took possession of all the keys. This was the first intimation of the presence of our force, or even of the existence of our expedition.

Between Griquatown and here we made two of the heaviest marches I've known yet. The wonder is we did not drop off our horses. After each march, without resting, we started, immediately the day broke, to perform a long day's heavy work.

When we got to Orange River we found that Tommy Atkins had been there before us and had broken up all the ponts and cut down all the lines. He did not, however, thereby prevent our crossing, for we swam across sufficient men, horses, and arms to guard the opposite bank and then set to work to get things into order.

Your humble servant was one of the second band to cross at 4 a.m. Four men placed their guns upon a rough wooden float together with the sub-commandant and swam across with it. They stormed the pont-keeper's house in their shirts, Berserker fashion, securing him and two other men and four natives before they got out of their beds, thus cutting off all means of communication with the enemy. At sunrise the Chief Commandant mounted the plank, and I, together with three others, put our guns on board and swam across, pushing it along.

From that moment, for the next two and a half days, I went stark naked backwards and forwards through the river and in the water, together with about a hundred others, working to construct an efficient ferry.

We had no tools but our hands, and no science but what we had learned from ox wagons. But on the morning of the third day we were in full swing, taking our wagons across. On the evening of the same day we started, about thirty strong, made a rapid and most arduous night march over forty miles of Karroo, reaching Prieska, our objective, as already related, at dawn.

The people here are coming up like trumps. Already we are growing strong, and if our anticipations continue to have the same fulfilment as hitherto, we shall shortly command an army as strong as any of the others at our chief bases.

Thomas Atkins has not yet come upon us, though we are in daily expectation that he will come in great force to give us Hades. We came here to fight and we're ready for him. We're not much to look at—a mere trifle—but we're here on business and have the pull over our enemy; because this is a howling wilderness, where the enemy can never travel fast, or in large numbers, or with heavy equipment. Nothing can exist here but a Boer or a Basuto pony.

You say to a man "Is hier Veld?"

"Ja! banja!"

"Waar?"

"Daarn," with an extensive sweep of the arm.

You lie down on your tum-jack so as the better to discover the grass and also to see if the stones perhaps possess some nutritive quality. Then he says "Kyk hier, man, Kyk hier!" and indicates a thing bristling with about forty varieties of thorns such as perforate the leather breeches of an Artillerist.

Then the local horses come along and skoff that bush entirely and wax fat and rich.

Man! I wish you were here! We want you badly in the organization of the newly proclaimed districts, as well as for the fighting. You could come all the way down in a cart, as several others did, though I personally preferred to ride all the time. You could still come, if you could get through. We are now about fifty hours (three hundred and fifty miles) from Bloemfontein, and we shall be another fifty before we finish unless the English come and wipe us out.

We are entirely without news, but I understand our people have Arundel, Naauwpoort, and Hanover.

While I was lying in the trenches at Magersfontein I had as a neighbour in the next trench Wally Coleman, of Bloemfontein, your cousin. He is Veldcornet of Bloemfontein and reputed, or rather proved, one of the bravest of our officers. When the war broke out he returned to Bloemfontein from Port Elizabeth, where he had latterly been living, and volunteered just after the first battle of Colenso; he told me he had heard from his Mother that poor old Percy Greathead had been killed down with the I.L.H. in Natal. He did not know where or on what occasion. (All these were old school fellows at St. Andrew's, Bloemfontein. It is pathetic to see them ranged in deadly war on different sides, whilst still the old boyish friendship lingers amongst them.—Ed.)

I ain't going to write you no more after this, so there! The present letter has exhausted my capacities "quite entoirely." Did you ever get the letter sent to you from Modder River before New Year? If so you never answered it. I am with Commandant Steenekamp and General Liebenberg. The movements of the former will always be mine, till we get knocked out. As yet there is no post to us, though later on there may be.

The Prieska Expedition (1900)

You will be sorry to hear I have lost that stout pony with the lovely frills sticking out of his ears, of which he was so proud; the one I brought from Jeppestown. It was the stoutest hearted little horse I ever bestrode, and perfect in every respect. He seemed absolutely incapable of fatigue. One day I galloped him a four hours' ride and he carried me many patrols. Coming down here I brought him and another along, and when we were lying that week at Modderriver he caught disease and had to be left behind. I expect he was too particular about the thorns he ate and the thorns took it amiss.

How's Master Robin? (his favourite horse— Ed.) I hope he's well. At any cost save him from the commando. I'm entitled to immunity for him as being on service at the front. Mr. Trijpe ought to be here; he'd get more skoff than he could eat.

I suppose the old span in the Specials (police) is getting less and less as they are drafted off to the front from time to time. Wannenberg, I saw by the paper, had gone to Natal. I do not even know if you are at home, but I write on the chance. Remember me to White, Plumacher, P. Louw, Eisenberg, and others who may still be there.

I do not anticipate that you will see me back before the end of the war. We have burnt our boats behind us and must go through, and what's more, we are going to do it.

I'm thankful for this hard work and constant excitement. It keeps one's mind occupied. If I repose for a week, the old trouble begins and I find it necessary to take four watches of night duty, instead of one.

Hope the Mater (mine) is keeping up.

I am very thankful for the service you have been to her. It is now nearly a month since I heard from her, as our letters were the last forwarded.

I trust your wife, mother, and little ones are all well and happy. Give my very kindest remembrances to them. Some day when we meet again you can acknowledge this letter. With very kindest regards, etc.

(Sgd.) F. R. MOSTYN CLEAVER.

Prieska,
March 7th, 1900.

My dearest Mother,

I am still here and keeping in excellent health and spirits.

Little or nothing happens. This is a quiet village compared to which Senekal is wildly exciting. I have been pretty busy with the work for which I came here. Of that naturally I can entrust nothing to paper. Some day, when the history of our expedition comes to be written, it will afford matter for wonder and admiration.

I leave here to-day or to-morrow. I am not at liberty to tell you where I go, except to state that it is westward, and—which will doubtless be a relief to you, though I myself don't much care—further and further away from all bullets.

We had a bit of an action yesterday near Britstown, about nine hours from here. The sound of cannon was strange to us, after not hearing it for so long. I took no part, as I was sent away with important despatches.

We have received reports how that Cronje was captured. It is a bit of a blow to our party, but not fatal, and our men are not discouraged by it. The successes gained by our other division around Kimberley are of great value.

Do not alarm yourself about me. I am living a life of rustic simplicity and quiet, and have nothing to do with fighting. I do not yet see any prospective date of returning home. When peace comes to Johannesburg I will come too.

You will from now probably not hear from me again, or only at rare intervals, for I am going away from the commandoes and the line of despatch riders. Hitherto I have written every week and hope you have had my letters.

I was greatly grieved to hear of the death of Oom Naas Ferreira (Commandant of the Western Division). It is a blow to the whole cause.

If you write to Nancy and Lily give them my love. I have not received any of your letters since Feb. 1st, but doubtless you are well. Don't be alarmed about me. I was never further out of danger than now.

Remember me to Robin, Jim, and Sambo. See that you go to Sheppard, Styx, Louis Jacobsz, or Smuts if you want assistance. Why don't you go to Pretoria and stay with Styx for a week? Try it, it'll do you good.

I should be glad to be with you again for a bit, but until my duty in this war is over I must subordinate all private desires. With my very best love, my dear Mother,

Your affectionate son,
REG.

Letters followed at intervals, dated Kenhardt and Upington, and then ceased altogether.

To my sister at Durban, Natal.

Kenhardt,
March 13th, 1900.

My dear Let,

I have, through the kindness of Mr. O. C., English magistrate of Upington, whom we are sending across our lines under passport, the opportunity of writing to you. I am at this moment at Kenhardt, in the Western Province, in the capacity of burgher and legal adviser to the Republican forces at present invading this part of the Cape Colony.

I do not know whether you have been able to hear from Mother since the year began. I last heard from her on Jan. 27th, when I penetrated into these western wilds, and have since had no letters forwarded. I write frequently per despatch rider, but do not know if the letters reach her.

I was Assistant Veldcornet and Chief of Special Police in Jeppestown during the first two months of the war.

On December 17th I left for the front as a volunteer, and went to Magersfontein, where I joined the Ladybrand Commando under Oom Naas Ferreira.

I lay for six weeks in the trenches, and then came away down here.

My experiences have been many and varied, but I have not time to write them now. My health is perfect, and all my former activity, endurance, and horsemanship have returned. I have never actually been in a battle, though frequently in close proximity to one. I have frequently been out on patrols, and under the shells during bombardments. That was when I was doing ordinary duty as trench burgher and patrol rider. But now as legal adviser I have not to fight, or be where fighting is, unless it happens by accident.

Our good faithful friend, Oom Naas Ferreira, who was lately elected Commander-in-Chief of the O. F. S. Western Army, was killed by an accident from his own gun—shot through the breast—during the late British advance on Kimberley. This is one of the saddest losses of the war. Many gaps have been made among our friends, but on the whole our losses have been miraculously small. Fanie Hauptfleisch, Chris Botha's brother-in-law, was shot through the breast at Magersfontein. Jan Botha was chased several miles by Lancers at Rooilaagte, but escaped.

Have you heard of O'F——? My last news of him was when T. V—— met him in Ladysmith, after Elandslaagte.

There are many friends in Johannesburg to keep an eye on Mother, and she had money in the bank belonging to me to live upon; but she pines dreadfully. I do not know when I shall see home again. I might at will have returned long ago; but I have no desire to do so as long as there is a blow to be struck for the Cause. Our people are still full of hope and courage and not demoralized, as represented by the Cape and Natal papers.

I am writing to Nancy by this same opportunity.

With very best love to you, believe me, my dear sister,

Truly your affectionate brother,
REG.

This letter reached Durban on the 25th March.

It is a pleasant incident, two men ranged on opposite sides, enemies technically, thus exchanging courteous deeds of kindness.

CHAPTER IV

ON TO KENHARDT AND BACK TO THE RAND

Kenhardt, O.V.S.
12th March, 1900.

My dearest Mother,

OU see I am now still further west. I have been sent hither by my Commandant upon an errand connected with our work here, which I cannot more specially relate to you, not knowing into whose hands this may fall. So far all is going well with us. We are favourably received by the population, and hope for greater things from this expedition. I may have to go still further west and even beyond the territory at present annexed by us, and away from opportunities of sending you news. But do not become anxious. I am in no danger.

Our influence now extends along the whole northern districts of the late Cape Colony, including Prieska, Upington, and Kenhardt, as far west as the borders of the German territory, whence we may reach a port, and so secure supplies of ammunition. But so far, having met with no opposition, we have done no fighting. Only we have heard that some scouts belonging to the south-western force have encountered a party of Kitchener's men, with whom they have had a brush, leaving seven of the enemy wounded on the veld, whilst our own casualties were nil.

I am now about one hundred miles further west than our main commando, accompanied by only two men. My return is uncertain. My thoughts are often with you, but my duty must be done.

> Believe me, my dearest Mother,
> Truly your affectionate son,
> (sgd.) REG.

After this for some time silence. The "Standard and Diggers' News" was singularly reticent. Scarcely a word appeared with reference to the Prieska Expedition. But one day, the 16th of April, the following telegram was handed me:

Viertienstroom.
Cleaver aan Cleaver Johannesburg.
Ben allhier aangekomen frisch en gezond, na een ry van 100 mylen door de woestyn. Ben wat moe. Verwach my spoedig. Het een vreeselyke honger en dorst. Kan banje koffy en koekjes verteer.

(All well and in good health after a ride of one hundred miles through the desert. Somewhat

To Kenhardt and back to the Rand

weary. Expect me soon. Very hungry and thirsty. Able to consume much coffee and cakes.)

A few days later another telegram from Klerksdorp ran:

Coming by to-morrow afternoon's train. Het banje verlangen na de lekker goed van my ma.

This was followed by another:

Fourteen Streams.   Cleaver.
Mrs. Cleaver
Care of Chief Detective.   17th April 1900.
I reached here yesterday safely, being the very last to leave our most forward positions in the Colony My retreat was cut off and I was compelled to make a long detour through the Kalahari and Langsberg. Health and spirits excellent. Wire me to-day, or to-morrow, to Fourteen Streams. How are you. Love.

The allusion to "coffee and cakes" and my "lekker goed" was because there was a standing feud between us on these heads. He alleging that I was never satisfied with the extent of his appetite, and I that he never did justice to my cookery!

On that day I was early busy in my pantry, preparing a feast to do honour to his return. When the time for the arrival of the train drew near Thomas inspanned and drove me, full of excitement, to the station. As the train drew up I ran from window to window, anxiously looking in. But no Reg was there. In great disappointment I called out his name again at the last carriage, when a gray head looked out and told me he had disembarked at Braamfontein station with his horses. Thither I drove, but found him not. So homewards I went, sadly disappointed, and just as I reached the door two ragged, shabby, toilworn figures, with rifle and bandolier, mounted on nags that fairly staggered under them, came in sight. "Well, Mother! hoe gaat het!" was the greeting, accompanied by a laugh at my astonished look.

We were each on the ground and in each others arms the next moment. I fear our joy at meeting somewhat interfered with due honour being done to my feast.

His companion was a young German who had fled from Prieska on the news of Kitchener's approach, and whom he had encountered in the desert and brought hither with him. The rescued one's loving reverence for the "doctor," as they were accustomed to entitle my son, was touching.

In the "Standard and Diggers' News" of 23 April 1900 appeared the following:

"Advocate Mostyn Cleaver has returned to the Rand, full of Prieska and Gordonia and colonial rebellion. His long, straggling personality,

To Kenhardt and back to the Rand

once so familiar in the Circuit Court and at the clubs, the semaphoric gesture of the large arm, the benevolent beam of Six-foot-Six from under the binoculars, now framed and shaded by a fair and fertile bush of 'takhaar' crop, swooped down upon me yesterday (writes a representative), breathing the Veld, Prieska, and patriotism. Fresh from the centre of Colonial revolt, to whom could one better appeal for a succinct narrative of what will be known in history as the 'Prieska Trek,' details of which had hitherto reached an inquisitive populace in scrappy numbers, lacking coherence and sequence. One might be sure to obtain at least legal accuracy from the forensic Six-foot-Six, and a tale told palatably and intelligibly.

"'The undertaking known as the "Prieska Expedition,"' commenced Mr. Cleaver, with the gravity of a lawyer in military riding breeches, 'was a joint Free State and Transvaal operation conducted under the name and authority of the Free State.

"'About the last Friday in January a complement of 150 men left Cronje at Magersfontein. They were under the command of General Piet Liebenberg, and their destination was ——'

"'Well?'

"'M'yes. The force was accompanied by two guns, a Krupp and a Nordenfeld-Maxim. Lukas Petrus Steenekamp of Venterstad, C.C., who had already won distinction at Stormberg, was appointed Assistant Hoofd Commandant, and joined the expedition a week later on the banks of the Riet River, near Douglas.

"'There being no legal adviser attached to the force, the late Hoofd Commandant Ferreira (who subsequently met so tragic a fate at Paardeberg) ordered me to report myself to General Liebenberg and Commandant Steenekamp, and to join the force in that capacity.

"'On February 8th our total force assembled at Douglas, one hundred and seventy-five men, strengthened by the guns already mentioned, and under the joint command of Assistant Hoofd Commandant Steenekamp, Vecht General Liebenberg, and Commandant B. J. Schutte of Kroonstad.

"'The object of the trek was presumably to enter the Western Province of the Cape Colony for purposes of raising burghers to assist us in our cause, and to proclaim the district Free State Territory. Hoofd Commandant Steenekamp proceeded in advance from Douglas to Zwemkuil on the Orange River, accompanied by Commandant Schutte and a staff of twenty-five men. At Zwemkuil we found the pont had been stranded and the wire dropped to the bed of the river. But our burghers swam the stream at early dawn, seized the guardians of the pont while they were still in bed, and cut off the line of communication with the enemy.' (A bold and saucy thing for the mild and benevolent Mr. Cleaver to do!)

"'Yes. I have prosecuted men for mere indiscretions compared with that! But this is war, not child's play. A la guerre comme à la guerre, you know!

"'However,' continued Six-foot-Six, 'we were joined by five hundred Griqualanders, and for three days worked like Trojans up to the neck in water to restore the pont. It was a quaint sight to see hundreds of our Federal friends in the "Altogether" driving troops of horses through, hauling ropes and wire, dragging beams and floats, and putting into the operation every artifice that Boer ingenuity could suggest to get the pont into working order. For three days I, myself, was clad only in a towel, a Mauser, and a pair of spectacles.'

"'Great Sartor! Really!!!'

"'Indeed! my clothes had been made "buit" by a sportive young burgher, who wished to see his "nooi," and who had left his wedding garments on the opposite bank. The men worked with such a will that, on the evening of the third day, the pont was in full working order, and the Hoofd Commandant and staff crossed to the Colonial side.

"'The Krijgsraad assembled and decided that he should proceed to Prieska, five hours further down (thirty miles) while the Griqualanders held the pont and awaited the arrival of General Liebenberg with the rest of the force.

"'All through the night of the 15th and 16th of February we plodded on through the deep sandy road. It was a grim forced march. Both man and beast were deadly tired and fit to drop; but the object to be gained was to surprise Prieska by daybreak.

"'The burghers behaved themselves with exemplary patience and fortitude, and not a murmur was heard, though many were scarcely able to keep the saddle from the fatigue of the last few days.

"'So well did we succeed that, when at dawn our advance guard entered Prieska, not only was our approach unknown to the English, but they were even unaware of our presence at Zwemkuil. The cry passed through the town, "Daar kom de Boere!" And when the officials came in their pyjamas to look they were politely but firmly requested to give up the keys. I may state that they subsequently expressed their high appreciation of the courtesy with which they were treated by the Boers: such was also the sentiment voiced at all places we went to.

"'At 8.30 a.m. February 16th, Hoofd Commandant Steenekamp (van de O.V.S. Leger, Afdeeling Westelyke Provinsie) proclaimed the district of Prieska Orange Free State Territory.

"'A meeting of the inhabitants was called that same afternoon; but the notice being too short, a further meeting was announced for Monday, February 19th.

"'All British subjects were given eight days in which to quit, or to agree to the proclamation and become burghers of the Orange Free State.

"'On Monday the 19th, at 4 p.m., the meeting took place, and the majority passed a vote agreeing to the proclamation. A committee of five local residents was appointed as a Krijgscommissie, and one of their number was nominated Landdrost, viz., Mr. Frans Smeer, now a refugee in our midst. Prior to that I had been Acting Landdrost, which position I now vacated.

"'The inhabitants of Prieska received us with open arms and responded pluckily to the commandeering, which was immediately begun. In a week's time between two hundred and fifty and three hundred burghers of that district had been placed under arms and had joined our commando, under their own commandant and field-cornets. The burghers of Prieska, as also those of Kenhardt and Upington are a very fine class of men, active, intelligent, and brave. I subsequently saw them ride into battle, and one could not have desired greater promptitude and keenness from our best Rustenburger or Krugersdorper.

"'The great cause of Afrikanderdom, the unity of the race from Capetown to the Zambesi, the mighty principle for which we are now struggling, they entertain, with an intensity which is unsurpassed even in the Republics. Without hesitating, when they had all to lose and less than we to gain, they unanimously obeyed the call to arms and threw in their lot with ours. As a class, moreover, I found them to be men who knew what they were fighting for, and who would be carried through and supported by convictions where mere animal courage would fail. The day upon which we were compelled to quit these brave allies and leave them to the vengeance of the enemy was a black-letter day for every one of us.

"'Within ten days of the proclamation of Prieska we had all the burghers in the field, and General Liebenberg had taken up a strong position at Hornwater, Dr. Smartt's farm, nine hours (fifty-four miles) from Prieska, upon the Britstown road. A strong patrol of seventy men had been placed between Prieska and Hopetown, and another patrol was stationed on the south-west.

"'From Prieska Mr. Koos Jooste and Mr. Andries de Wet, the cyclists of more peaceful times, were dispatched to Kenhardt under the titles of Commandant and Assistant Commandant, to proclaim that district. They reached Kenhardt on the early morning of February the 28th, and were very nearly overwhelmed in an ambuscade of Bastaards, who fired upon them in the dark at a distance of eight yards. Fortunately they escaped and, playing a bold hand, were masters of the town before 8 a.m. They then posted up the Orange Free State Proclamation.

"'About this time we began to get news from across the English border of the surrender of General Cronje. We passed a time of feverish anxiety and uncertainty. At that stage already the fearful rumours which reached us almost

To Kenhardt and back to the Rand 91

caused a panic among the Colonials. Nor was it in fact until we returned to Griqualand and the South African Republic that we got possession of the whole detailed truth.

"'On the morning of the 6th March the English advanced out of Britstown towards Hornwater, against us, with a force of four or five hundred men. The troops comprised City of London Volunteers and a portion of another regiment, with a battery of artillery. General Liebenberg went out with one hundred and seventy-five to two hundred men, one Krupp gun, and one Maxim Nordenfeld to meet them. After a whole morning's fight he succeeded in completely routing them, with a loss on their side of between seventy and one hundred men, including seven prisoners. We lost two men and had three wounded.

"'We pursued the enemy several miles, and had it not been that our horses and men were even more fatigued than theirs, we must eventually have taken more prisoners, and possibly some of their guns.

"'The next morning the British evacuated Britstown, where they had been previously entrenched, and returned to De Aar.

"'It was curious to note the frame of mind of the prisoners, who doubtless expected to be killed and eaten by the savage bearded Boer. One of them went down on his knees and wildly implored General Liebenberg not to roast him alive. He was considerably reassured when the General, in response, gave him a pull at his flask. He subsequently became a sort of pet in the laager, where he made great strides in inspanning oxen and cracking the whip.

"'On the Saturday Hoofd Commandant and staff went to Kenhardt where matters were already getting under way. During the ensuing week the burghers came up and five hundred took the field. The enthusiasm here was even greater than at Prieska.

"'On March the 5th, or thereabouts, Commandant Jooste had proclaimed Upington and the district of Gordonia, on the mouth of the Orange River, and in the following week Hoofd Commandant Steenekamp followed him thither.

"'At Upington the burghers were equally enthusiastic, and the lists showed a rally of three hundred who were able to go into the field. They were, however, never called out, since we shortly after received our orders to return across the Orange River.

"'It was while at Upington that I was sent by Hoofd Commandant Steenekamp to Prieska, with important dispatches and instructions. The distance is twenty-four hours (one hundred and forty-four miles) on horseback. When eight hours (forty-eight miles) from Prieska, I met some burghers coming from there, who told me that the Transvaalers had crossed the river into Griqualand on Saturday (it was now Tuesday), and that the English were in possession of Prieska, and also of the pont, and that all the Prieska burghers had fled to their homes.

"'I had thus no alternative but to turn off and make for Kenhardt, a distance of sixteen hours (ninety-six miles) inland, where I hoped to find some of the Colonials still on foot. Here again I was disappointed. I found that the Krijgscommissie of Kenhardt had disbanded the burghers, in spite of the brave and determined efforts of V. C. Jan Borrius of Potchefstroom and V. C. Hermann Judilwitz of Makwassie, Z. A. R. to keep them together.

"'I also learned that the Hoofd Commandant and staff had quitted Upington and proceeded along the north bank of the Orange River towards Griqualand. The Krijgscommissie of Kenhardt, or rather a portion of them, had gone to surrender themselves to the English, and had taken with them two of our men, Herbe Jooste and Jakobus de Wet (O. V. S.), as prisoners and hostages.

"'Jan Borrius, Hermann Judilwitz, an artillerist named Koenij, and myself were thus the only Transvaalers left, with the exit barred at Prieska, the Colonials dispersed and the English advancing. A number of young Colonials expressed their intention of leaving the Colony, and asked us to take them across. Together we formed a party and struck out for Upington, which we succeeded in reaching in safety. There we effected a crossing and took a couple of days' rest. The situation was rather critical;

for our whole party numbered but thirty, while we had certain information that one thousand English were on their way to Upington, some even said commanded by Kitchener in person, breathing vengeance against "the man with the English name." Also that British reinforcements were on their way to cross the river higher up, and so cut us off.

"'We concluded, therefore, not to travel up the river bank, but to strike off immediately to the north and cross the Kalahari Desert. This we succeeded in doing in the course of a week. And not a bit too early; for the advance guard of the enemy, so we subsequently heard, actually crossed the river at a point so as to intercept our way, had we kept the river bank; while another body had followed us up from behind.

"'We did not care much about the Tommies once we had plunged into the desert; our principal danger was from the Bastaard population, through the midst of whom we had to travel. The British Government makes pets of them and plays them off against the Boers in that part of the Colony. They are well armed, and a body of five or six hundred could be called together at short notice. The British had used them to ambush us at Kenhardt, and might do so again here.

"'Prieska, Kenhardt, and Upington are now all in possession of the English, and will not again be accessible to a scouting party of one hundred and sixty burghers. But the vast probabilities held out by the Western Province are worth the expedition of a far greater force.

"'It took me nearly a month to traverse the whole distance from the Western Province to Fourteen Streams; and from the time the break up began, until I reached Johannesburg, I travelled a distance of one hundred and thirty-four hours on horseback (eight hundred and four miles).

"'When once the enemy was evaded and circumspected the chief opposing force was thirst. On one occasion we had ridden two days and a night without meeting water. Our beasts and ourselves were equally done up. A small excrescence in the plain, which the natives dignify with the name of a kopje, appeared in the distance. Urged to exertion by hope, we spurred on to it. Alas! we found nothing. Unable to move on, we sat down—to die.

"'But a young German, whom we had come across in the desert flying for his life from Prieska, and taken into our party, had become devoted to me, whom he looked upon as his rescuer. If effort of his could find water, I should have it. So he clomb the "kopje," telling us, if he found water, he would fire his revolver. After a sufficiently long absence the welcome shot was heard. We rushed in its direction and succeeded in getting most of the precious fluid down our parched throats before our horses discovered what we were about. To

Rudolf Meyer is due that our little band escaped a dreadful death by thirst.

"'I think I may reasonably claim, by virtue of experience, to set up as a competent judge of the flavours of respective kinds of tadpoles. I have struggled with mules and horses who should get the biggest share out of a Kalahari puddle, and I can aver that the flavour of a nine months' dead sheep is more palatable than that of one which died in the drinking place only a fortnight ago.

"'The Prieska Expedition is past and over. It will be a subject for later enquiry to ascertain the various causes which led to its termination. But one thing even now stands clear, and that is: the súpremacy of Great Britain in South Africa was never so seriously assailed, during the whole war, as in that undertaking. England has reason to congratulate herself that it is a thing of the past; for the wave of revolt was in a good way to spreading like fire throughout the whole Colony, and the field of possibilities was infinite.'"

My son reached home just after the Begbie explosion, whilst the town was red-hot with horror and determined to sacrifice *someone* to appease its indignation.

He did not join in the popular cry against the man whom the authorities had seen proper to arrest as the perpetrator; but held to the entire belief in the impossibility of his guilt.

To Kenhardt and back to the Rand

Nor did he remain satisfied with the expression of an opinion merely, but visited the unlucky one in prison and exerted himself strenuously in his behalf.

He had at that time a few days of well-earned "verlof" to rest a little both himself and horses. One of the poor beasts died from exhaustion, but the other, which had carried him all through the desert to and from Prieska, showed his grit by refusing absolutely to die.

After a fortnight's rest, when my son went into the field again to take up the post of Commandant of the Scouts along the Vaal River, he took "Ou Baas" with him, but had to send him back to me for further rest, as he was absolutely unequal tó the work.

Poor Ou Baas! I fed him on green barley, and manna and mealies—whatever I could get, and coaxed him by giving him his food little by little out of my hand. I had almost despaired of his recovery when, one morning as I came into his stall holding out a few stalks of green barley, as I patted him, he turned on me his eyes, with a little of their former fire and gave a gentle chuckle of recognition. After this he gained strength. On the Sunday before Lord Roberts's arrival, that is on the 27th of May, 1900, there was a frantic commandeering of men and horses, of which very few were left in town. They were wanted to go out to fight at Klip River. I trembled for Ou Baas, but resolved not to part with him lightly. Had not my son said I must get him ready for him as he might urgently require him? So when the commandeering official knocked at the door and demanded Ou Baas, I said I could not give him as my son wanted him down at the Scouts' laager at any hour.

"But we *must* have him. There are no horses to speak of in town and we cannot spare *one* for any service." And he held up his revolver as if he would intimate his intention of taking poor Ou Baas *vi et armis*.

"Oh!" said I, "you needn't hold up that thing. I have a revolver too; and you are not going to have my son's horse."

In the end I was for the moment victorious. The next morning at 9 a.m. I was down at the Court House with a request for protection for Ou Baas.

"Of course you were right to refuse," said Mr. v. d. B. "They can't take your son's horse. He may want it any moment for urgent duty." And he gave me a certificate of exemption for Ou Baas.

But "the best laid plans——"

The British occupied Johannesburg on Thursday 31 May. Their poor beasts were in a ghastly condition, staggering under the weight of their riders, and literally dying like flies.

So it was announced that no one of the citizens could retain his horse, except by special permission of the remount officer, upon cause shown.

To Kenhardt and back to the Rand

I spanned in poor Ou Baas, who was by this time getting on fairly, and drove to the Court House. Having made my way upstairs through crowds waiting around, I, after some time, obtained admission to the office. In the anteroom was a man, a Hollander, a former inferior official of the old government. Once when I used to go to that building, none more officious than he to show me attention. But to-day *he did not know me*. Ultimately, seeing no chance of admission to the inner office, I preferred my request for poor Ou Baas's exemption in writing.

Believing it would facilitate my request, I wrote that the horse I desired to keep *could* be of no value for work, as he was but just home, after having carried a heavy man a thousand miles. I believe that sealed his doom. Just as I reached home a young officer stopped the trap, unharnessed the horse, and carried him off. And that was the last I saw of Ou Baas. I had snatched him from the jaws of Scylla, only to fall into those of Charybdis. A week or two later they gave me fifteen pounds compensation for him. He was worth his weight in gold.

CHAPTER V
THE LAST EFFORT

ON the night of Tuesday, 29 May 1900, about seven o'clock, just as we were going to dinner, I heard a cry, " Oh, Sister! Here's a burgher!"
Running hastily to see what it might mean, strong arms were thrown around me and I was folded to the breast of my son.

"Dearest, you are just in time for dinner. Come in, for I know you are famished. And let Thomas off-saddle your horse."

"Mother, I have only fifteen minutes' leave. Do not let us waste time in eating."

He led me back into the sitting-room and we sat down, he still holding me close to him.

"Mother, I have come to say good-bye. Lord Roberts is at Germiston; our commandoes are at Langlaagte. All is lost now! Our last stand will be Pretoria, and there, as I can no longer live for my country, I will die with it."

I spoke of his pure British blood, bade him think of it and of me and surrender.

"Yes, Mother, my blood is British, but Africa is my native land and my whole heart belongs to it. Had I a thousand lives I would freely give them all for the freedom of Africa. You are different. England is your native land, and you do right to love it and stand up for it. But Africa is mine, Mother! it is a bitter thing to see Chamberlain take away my country's independence."

"But, my dearest, it is not altogether Chamberlain's work. The Republican Government has been much to blame."

"Mother, do not speak of this Government" (this with an accent of rage and indignation); "it is the most infamous that ever existed under the sun. It was bound to bring down God's curse on the land, and it has brought it."

"But why then did you fight for it?"

"Never, *never* have I fired a shot for the Government. But for *Africa!* Had it been possible for us Afrikanders to win in this war we would have made of Africa a nation as good as Britain."

"Impossible ambitions" truly!

Kneeling beside him, with my arms round his neck and my head on his bosom and his dear arms closely embracing me, we each asked and received pardon from the other for all offences. And then it was time to part.

Then he mounted his horse after a last embrace, and went slowly down the street, still calling out of the darkness "Good-bye, Mother, good-bye," until he turned into another street and I could hear him no more.

I did not know until later that he had been sent on a service of special danger; namely, to get away the last gun and ammunition that remained in the town. This he safely effected.

Lord Roberts entered the town, and the commandos hastened on to dispute his entrance into Pretoria.

I heard nothing of or from him for many days. Pretoria was occupied, Kruger and his officials escaping and carrying off the public chest with them, as well as a goodly number of the British prisoners of war. But of the fate of my son I could get no word until, on the morning of the 18th of June, Willie Begbie came in with the news that a friend of his, just in from Pretoria, had told him my boy was safe, but a prisoner. He had seen him in the custody of a file of soldiers marched down the street to the office of Major Poore.

Whilst Begbie was still speaking I heard a cry of joyful surprise, and running into the hall, found my dear son standing there, in soiled and tattered garments, laughing gaily at the exclamations his appearance had called forth.

"Here I am, Mother!" he cried, as I threw my arms around him, "I hardly thought you would know me in this disguise. One of my own men down at the station just now pretended *he* didn't!"

Later he gave me the events of the last ten days.

The Last Effort

On the night he left me he, with about forty-one of his men, got the last gun out of Johannesburg and a wagon-load of ammunition. On a slight ascent near Braamfontein station the wagon upset, and not daring to strike a light, he and his men went down on hands and knees and felt about in the grass to pick up the ammunition, moving as silently as they could. It was just gray dawn when the last cartridge was picked out of the grass. Then they set off on the road to Pretoria. But it was not long before they were perceived, or imagined they were, by the enemy. At the distant sight of horse the small commando put spurs to their steeds, and it was *Sauve qui peut!* Then he spurred in front of the fugitives, upbraiding, imploring, conjuring them not to disgrace their manhood by abandoning their gun and officer. But on every such panic his small escort grew less. However, he got his gun to Pretoria at last, and was able to take part in the fighting there. How a shell burst within five yards of him, how his ankle was injured, and how he managed to struggle off the field and find refuge in the house of his friend Advocate Stockenström, at Sunnyside, one of his letters relates.

Walking, aided by his stick and his friend's arm, in the garden a few days later, an English officer passed and spoke to him. This officer being, with Afrikander hospitality, asked into the house, accepted a whisky and soda, and whilst chatting amicably said to Veldcornet

Mostyn Cleaver, "I suppose you have had enough of fighting by now and are glad to be here?"

"I beg your pardon; I regret nothing so much as my inability to be with my comrades in the field, whom my wound prevents me joining."

"Do you talk like that, my fine fellow!" and calling a piquet of soldiers he ordered them to march him before Major Poore, to whom he sent a note saying my son was a dangerous person.

Questioned by Major Poore, my son said: "Major Poore, if you will give me my gun and put me over your lines, telling me I could go with honour, wounded as I am, I shall try to reach my comrades and still fight for my country."

The Major, unlike the previous officer, saw nothing wrong or dangerous about my son, but offered to take his *parole* and send him back to his friend. He asked if there were anything else he would like.

"Yes," replied my son, "my Mother is in Johannesburg and knows nothing of my fate, and I know she is anxious. I should like to send her word."

"You may carry the message yourself," said the Major. Thus he was sent to me.

I asked him what he thought of British soldiers now he had seen them at close quarters.

"Mother," he said heartily, "Tommy Atkins is the finest fellow under the sun. I shall never forget how kindly they treated me going up to Major Poore's quarters. They kept asking if they were walking too quickly for my lame foot, and accommodating their pace to mine, showing the greatest respect all the the time."

"And the officers?"

"They are thorough gentlemen. To be sure the one who arrested me after drinking and chatting pleasantly may be called an exception! And he comes from Glastonbury, too, where we had such happy times!"

His face and hands were full of small splinters of iron from a bomb that burst quite near him.

In the afternoon of the second day after his arrival he went down to the house of a Boer ambulance doctor to have the splinters extracted. The operations not being over before the hour at which he had to be indoors, he remained all night at the doctor's. My true friend Mr. Darragh felt anxious about this; but I had no fear, knowing the singleness of his heart and the steadfastness of his honour. This was on Thursday night.

On Friday, after dinner, a British volunteer officer, of whom my son had often said " he is a man of chivalrous honour," and whom he regarded with a strong feeling of friendship, came in and we all remained chatting over war incidents for some time.

At last I bade them good-night and went upstairs to bed. But hardly had I fallen asleep when a tap came on my door, and on enquiring "Who's there?" my son replied, "Mother, don't be alarmed, I have come to tell you I am arrested and must go at once down to the Commissioner's office."

I slipped on a dressing-gown and slippers and followed him downstairs. Inside the room door stood a man armed with a rifle, who was there to conduct him to the office. The Volunteer officer still sat on the sofa, as I had left him, beside my son.

The man sent to arrest him was one of my son's own former police, an Afrikander. He seemed much embarrassed and said in Dutch: "Jufvrouw, I am so sorry to have to arrest my old baas; but I am bound to obey."

"What is the reason of this?" I asked the officer.

"Don't be alarmed," he replied, "I am going with him to the Commissioner to see all about it."

On their return my son told me that Captain —— had stood security for him to surrender himself at the show ground the next morning at 9 o'clock. This was where the prisoners of war were kept previous to being sent off to Cape Town.

At 8.30 a.m. he stepped into a cab and at 9 a.m. entered the grounds a prisoner, never again to be a free man until released by the universal conqueror—Death.

The Last Effort

In the afternoon I sent up my Kafir boy, Thomas, with a few necessaries and a note to Colonel Wright asking permission to visit my son. He replied that no one was allowed to visit a prisoner without a special permit from the military governor of the town.

Mr. Darragh gave me on the Monday a letter to Colonel Mackenzie, the military governor, which I took personally. Long I had to wait in the corridor amongst a crowd of rough men, and when at last I induced an individual in uniform to take in my letter, it was returned after some time with the permission written across the corner.

It was Wednesday before I could get to the show ground. In the meantime William Begbie came to see me. It happened that as my son was brought by the guard to surrender his parole Begbie was speaking to the Captain. He went forward to meet him and shook hands, whereupon the Captain asked, "Do you know that fellow?"

"Yes, I know him well."

"And what kind of man is he?"

"A gentleman in every sense of the word!"

"But he's an Englishman and consequently a rebel!"

"Oh, no! He's a Free Stater born and a burgher and official of the Transvaal," replied Begbie.

"Oh! that makes all the difference." Begbie gave me his card and an introduction to this officer, from whom I received great courtesy. Begbie's word, for he was a *persona grata* with the military, was also of great service to my son.

Arrived at the gate of the show grounds my carriage was stopped by the guard and my permit sent up to Colonel Wright, who sent a speedy order for my admission and himself came down to meet me. I asked him to inspect a few things I had brought; but he replied: "Oh no, Mrs. Cleaver! I should not think of inspecting anything you bring! I have heard of you."

He brought me to his own room and sent for my son and then left us together. My son was anxious only about one thing; he had been told the British would bring him to trial as a rebel.

"I am willing to die as a loyal burgher," he said, "but I could not endure to stand as a felon in the dock!" He related what he had done at Prieska, Upington, and Kenhardt, how he had released the civil servants and allowed them to go free. Doubtless a generous error. The Magistrate of Prieska, meeting the mail cart, gave information of the occupation of the place, which, had they detained him prisoner, could not have reached Cape Town or the army for some time as these northern districts are so isolated.

On my return home I wrote to Bishop Gaul and to the Rev. Hon. A. V. Lyttelton, each of whom bore him great friendship, relating the one subject of his anxiety.

The Last Effort

They each wrote to Lord Roberts, testifying to his integrity and burghership. They were given an assurance that Lord Roberts intended to treat him as an honourable foe. But these letters did not reach him until he was in Ceylon.

On the Saturday morning early an orderly came over from Major Banon, the military commissioner of the district in which von Brandis Square fell, telling me a telephonic message had come to him that my son would be sent with other prisoners to Cape Town that day, and I might go to see him before he left.

On my arrival I found the departure had been delayed until the following morning, Sunday.

Colonel Wright received me and stayed chatting a little while. I remarked, if my dear son would have listened to me he would not now be a prisoner of war.

"Oh, but a man cannot take his political opinions from his Mother!" he said. "If your son saw that his duty led him to fight for the flag we have conquered, he had every right to do so. For myself, I believe Freedom and Justice live under *that* flag," pointing to the Union Jack, which waved outside, "and I will live and die for it."

After talking some time in the Colonel's room, we went outside and walked a long time in the grounds. He told me that the departure of the prisoners was deferred until the next day, because news had come in that a rescue was going to be attempted.

He felt the position of his country and his own acutely, but bore it bravely, even cheerfully. Yet once looking round on the hills, he cried, "Oh, Mother, it is hard—hard. Everything seemed at my feet. I could have been the first amongst my countrymen—and now—*to be here!*"

He saw the reality of the conquest of the Republics and spoke of what his future course should be after the near end of the war.

"I have recovered my love for rural life," he said, "I shall never live in the town again. When I return, you and I will take a farm and try to be happy once more." Although his broken ankle bone must have been very painful, he uttered never a word of complaint. Indeed, until I got his letters from Ceylon, I did not even know how serious it was.

We remained together until the edge of night. Only once more in this life were we to meet!

The next morning, Sunday, I was driven early by my Kafir boy to the show grounds. At one of the gates the sentinel came up to the carriage and with kindly sympathy bade me be of good cheer. "We have news to-day," said he, "that de Wet is taken, so we shall soon have peace and your son will come home."

When I reached the prisoners' quarters all were busy packing their small belongings for the journey. My son gave the mattress I had

The Last Effort

sent him the week before to the orderly who had been told off to wait upon him. I had brought a trunk packed with a good store of linen (he loved clean linen abundantly) and other clothing; also in a basket, a few luxuries for the railway journey.

The soldiers had already "fallen in," but owing to some report, which was not made known to the prisoners, the march down to Braamfontein station did not begin until noon. It was a gusty cold day. I drove after the procession of prisoners and soldiers, over the dilapidated street leading from the show grounds to Braamfontein station. Out of the cottages, as we passed, sprang forlorn women and children, weeping and shouting farewells. At the plantation my son was allowed to leave the ranks in order to help me across the lengthy stretch leading to the train. This stood some quarter of a mile up the line, beyond the station.

Just outside the grounds of the railway a weird throng of dishevelled women stood. All of the poorest class, some without any head covering and with dishevelled looks, they stood lamenting and crying out frantic farewells.

The rank and file of the prisoners were entrained first. My son, calm and self possessed, stood there giving in Dutch the directions of the soldiers. They treated all with the greatest kindness, and my son with the respect due to his rank. There were two German officers amongst the prisoners. I could not noticing the deference of their manner to my son. Eight cannon and several hundred men were going down to guard the train, as it was rumoured that a rescue was to be attempted.

The last to embark was my dear son. A sergeant came up and respectfully asked him if he would mind getting upon a truck for the few yards down to the station, where a first class carriage was awaiting him.

He stooped to me and kissed me, saying quite cheerfully, "Good-bye, Mother!" and hoisted himself on to a truck which was carrying a cannon.

The train moved off slowly. He stood up waving his hand. As it moved further away he climbed on to the gun carriage and waved his white handkerchief until the station hid him from my sight. And that was the last glimpse of him I shall ever have, until I meet him in Paradise!

I heard no news of him as the days rolled slowly by. A former "friend" (?) of his, a British Volunteer, I blush to say, came in and assured me that it was highly probable the prisoners would all be shot by the British, as a rescue was to be attempted. This "friend" at the same time "borrowed" my only vehicle and never returned it. He also "borrowed" about a thousand bundles of precious forage, remarking that "doubtless you commandeered it." In reality my son had bought it at highest

The Last Effort

market price from a British subject who had been ordered over the border, and who must have left it to perish but for this act of friendship.

On Sunday the 8th July, as I came out of church, the West Lancs. were drawn up in line ready for marching back to camp. Their Colonel, who had already shown us such chivalrous kindness, was standing before them. I, absorbed in sorrowful anxiety for my son, and forgetting all else, went up to him and asked: "Have you news of the prisoners—of my dear son?"

The Colonel took both my hands in his and replied: "They are all well and safely arrived in Cape Town. I will see that you get a letter from your son."

There are, one sees, British *and* British.

And this was the first letter I received, a pink placard was fastening the end upon which was printed "Opened under Martial Law."

Green Point Camp, Cape Town,
July 11th, 1900.

My dear Mother,

I got here in good order and condition on Friday last, after having been five days on the road. We had a very good journey down and were not visited by General de Wet, though I was told by the British officers on board the train that he was cruising around somewhere east of Kroonstad and "surrounded."

It was pretty pleasant travelling, and the

karroo was not inordinately hot at this season of the year.

On arriving here we were placed in the recreation ground at Green Point, which has been converted into a camp for our accommodation. Only Orange Free Staters are put in here, the Transvaalers being sent to Simon's Town and St. Helena.

All those Free Staters who were taken at Paardeberg are here. When I walked down the line of tents I might, for all the world, have been at Magersfontein in my old trenches, there were so many of the old Ladybrand Commando sitting in front of the tents. Wally Coleman, taken in de Villebois' last stand, Stephanus Ferreira, Frickie and Johannes van Reenen, are all among the number.

I do not know how long I shall be here, as I am expecting daily to be removed to the Simon's Town or St. Helena camp.

How long we shall be before we return home of course depends upon the duration of the war. I, for my part, hope our people will stand out another six or twelve months.

I saw McFadyan of Pretoria (an old pre-war acquaintance) whose wife is Mrs. Andrew Morice's sister. He came in to see me a couple of days ago and tells me Andrew has been very ill indeed for a long time. I have not heard of or seen Michael Farrelly, though the papers say he is back. I do not know anything about anybody else.

I hope you have been able to obtain trace of Robin. Even though we might be unable now to substantiate the claim, later on we shall still have the opportunity.

I can give you no certain address to write to just yet as I do not know my ultimate destination, but McFadyan is censor to our camp, and if you write here he would probably see that it was forwarded to me.

With very best love, believe me, my dearest Mother,
    Ever your affectionate son,
          REG.

CHAPTER VI
OFF TO CEYLON

S.S. "Mohawk,"
Off Durban,
July 20th, 1900.

My dearest Mother,

AM at this moment on board the SS. "Mohawk," bound for Ceylon along with some two hundred other Republicans as prisoners of war. We left Cape Town on Wednesday and expect to reach Durban to-morrow morning, where the Colonel has kindly promised to post our letters.

Ours is the first batch going to the new station. Tom Menton (Chief Detective) is one of our number. If you tell Richard Brink, he will inform Mrs. Menton.

We are travelling in great comfort. The burghers are forward with the soldiers, and the Krijgsofficieren enjoy the accommodation and privileges of first-class passengers, along with the British officers. I, as Veldcornet, fall under this latter category. The weather is fine and I am proving a better sailor than on any previous voyage. The Colonel, too, sees that we

Off to Ceylon

have everything we want, so I anticipate a prosperous journey.

I do hope you will have sufficient money to last you until I return. If you can succeed in letting the house it will render you quite safe. Do not, if you can possibly avoid it, pay any more money to the mortgagees. They have no right to demand any as long as the moratorium continues. When that ceases we can once more resume the payments as in duty bound; but anything you may pay them previous to that is merely an act of good-will on your part. (This moratorium was declared null and void some time after the conclusion of peace, causing much distress to us who were poor.)

You had better without delay send in a written claim for the return of Robin, or, in default, the sum of sixty pounds sterling. You remember I was offered eighty pounds cash for him quite recently. V., one of my old police, now one of the British valuators, and another valued him at respectively fifty and sixty. J., the old Jew butcher, who S. says saw him taken out of the stable by British officers on the night of the occupation of Johannesburg, lives near S.'s old residence. Get S. to face up in the matter. O'F. also will help you in the matter.

I hope Jim is duly ticketed and safe from the dog-catchers. A recent proclamation, too, requires bicycles to be registered. Do not forget to have mine fixed up.

There's my saddle, and bridle too, at S.'s, both very valuable, and as Paddy says "don't belong to me," but to G. A. H. Dickson, to whom I must render account. Please get them from S. even though you have to fetch them yourself.

You might let Styx know how and where I am. He'll be pleased to hear. It's not half bad sailing this sea in a great ship, but I'd give all I own to be sailing the Highveld under Louis Botha with my old mauser across my back. I have no more at present to write. Do not be alarmed about me for I am in excellent health and in good hands.

Remember me to O'Flaherty (former sub-editor of the "Leader").

With very best love and fond wishes to yourself, believe me, my dear old Mother,

Truly and affectionately your son,
REG.

Johannesburg,
21 Aug. 1900.

My very dear Son,

Yours of the 20th July from on board the "Mohawk" came (duly censored) to hand in the first days of the month, the Durban line being fairly open, although de Wet is very mischievous on that of the Cape. I have fulfilled or am fulfilling all your various directions. The dogs are ticketed, the bicycle registered, the saddle in the harness room. I have done all I can for the recovery of Robin as follows:

I went down to V. and C., the Government valuators, and formerly your own men, who had promised to find out all about Robin. They told me that after being taken away from the stable he had been given to a man called J——, who had been sent on duty to Heidelberg. Later they told me the poor horse had been badly wounded in the leg and left at Heidelberg. I was awfully sorry for our poor Robin, whom we had so carefully kept out of the wars. Anyway, I thought it best to speak to the military official and make a claim for his value. After two or three vain efforts to see Major Macpherson I was admitted to the presence of his secretary, or something of the kind, Lord Compton, to whom I made a distinct deposition that the horse is ours and all about him. Willie Begbie was with me, who is a *persona grata* with the military. I was very well received and asked to return next day, which I did with the same escort. But Lord C—— was very cool, and put us off without going further into the matter.

The day following Willie came to tell us that Lord C. had been told by V. and C. that the horse never was ours, but had been commandeered by you at the beginning of the war!!

Imagine your mother under such an accusation! I made Willie drive me down to the remount yard at once, and if V. and C. did not understand my powers of rhetoric previously *they do now.*

My next trip was to the Exploration Buildings, accompanied always by Willie, to interview the Major. I told him the whole matter, and in conclusion said: " Please understand, Major Macpherson, that, much as we love our Robin, I am not objecting to give him for the Queen's service. She should have ten horses if I had them; yes, and all I have. But I do object to the imputation of having made a false statement. I have brought with me Mr. Begbie, whom you know, to testify to our possession of the horse long before the war."

The Major noted what I said, and assured me that I should have the horse restored.

I repeated that if he were needed for the Queen's service I would give him willingly. But he replied, "No, you shall have your horse."

Begbie told me afterwards that Lord Roberts had given orders that the special favourite horse of any lady should be spared. Was it not like Lord Roberts? The Major said, " Mrs. Cleaver is a lady, and shall be treated as such."

About four days later I was walking down Commissioner Street when a trap driven by an officer stopped, and an orderly jumped off and came to me, saying Major Macpherson wished to speak to me. It was to ask me to be at the

Off to Ceylon

remount stables at 10 a.m. next day and to bring Begbie with me.

I took the precaution of bringing Thomas as well. You know how stupid *I* am at recognizing man or beast, but a Kafir is *never* mistaken.

As soon as we reached the yard the Major, who was very busy, called out to bring the horse.

He was led out by S.'s Kafir groom.

Thomas cried out with enthusiasm, "Bona, bona, inkosikaas! Robin!" and Willie said "Yes, it's your horse," whilst I, recognizing him at once, ran across the yard and put my arms round his neck, calling him by his name; and he gave a gentle little chuckle and smelt me lovingly over. He was in lovely condition, with never a sign of a wound, and beautifully groomed.

I said to the Kafir: "But where has he been all this time?"

To which he replied: "In baas S.'s stable!"

Yes, my son! Misfortune is the fire that shows of what metal friends are made.

And now our dear beautiful Robin, who loves us both so much, is safely munching what forage he can get in our stable; not too much, as —— has carried off nearly all the forage, saying, "He supposed I had commandeered it!" I told him I had bought it at a great price from a British subject who was put over the border, just to put a little money in his pocket.

This pleases you, my dearest, better than that Robin should be exposed to the bullets of your friends in the service of my Queen! Is that not a strange paradox when you and I are the dearest objects to each other on this earth? Alas! alas! for the tragedy of life!

Take care of your dear self, my last son of the three! Come back to me safe and sound.

Jim and Sambo are well. Jim goes up every night to Yeoville to see his mother and guard the house, and returns in the morning for his breakfast.

And so M. J. F. never came to see you! The Scot (McFadyan) was better than either of the Irishmen. —— came to see me a day or two after you left and kindly soothed my anxiety by telling, with a most vindictive look and manner, that should de Wet approach your train, the British officers would certainly shoot you all. Tell me, do I dream, or was it I that risked a good deal to enable him to escape before the war?

I knew of your safe arrival in Cape Town before your letter came. As we left church on the Sunday morning I saw Colonel Wright, with his regiment standing all in a row, and went up to him asking if he had news of you, for oh! my dearest, I was so anxious. He put out his hand and took both mine and told me so nicely you were safely at Cape Town, and he would send me an address to write to. Was it not sweet of him?

God bless you, my very dear boy. Take care of your health. I need not tell you to remember

me, whose thoughts are with you every moment, sleeping or waking.
                    Your loving Mother.

Arrived at Dyatalawa Camp, he occupied himself—since he could no longer serve his country in the field—in doing what he could to benefit his fellow captives.

                    S.S. " Mohawk,"
                    Aug. 7th, 1900.

My dear Mother,
The time of this present writing is Tuesday, to which I affix the date of Aug. 7th at random. We crossed the line yesterday and to-day it is passing hot. This, in connection with the scenic effect of the ocean, strongly reminds me of my trip through the Kalahari Desert. Menton remarks the mealie lands are looking well all along the road, but I prefer the kafir koorn. Martinus doesn't like " die wereld." He says " die veld is te blauw " to agree with the sheep, and that " gansboerderij " would pay better.

I have as yet nothing to write you about. We expect to reach Colombo to-night late, when our letters will be posted to notify our safe arrival. We are being sent inland up the mountains to a place with an unpronounceable name and a healthy climate. Five hundred prisoners, who left Cape Town after us, but by a faster boat, will probably be there to welcome us on our arrival.

The voyage has been most pleasant, the sea

has not been too rough and head winds have kept the air cool all the time. I wrote you from Durban full instructions about the management of our affairs. In case you have not received that letter, I shall in a later one repeat my instructions. If you can spare it, I should like you to send me ten pounds. I do not know what our address will be, or what the method of remittance, but Colonel Mackenzie of Johannesburg will probably tell you all he can, for I hear him well spoken of. Menton is getting a remittance made to him too. Richard Brink will see you about it, and the two amounts can be combined.

If you succeed in letting the house and also in cashing the fifty pound note of the Kruger Government at some later date before I return, I should like you, if the rent is sufficient for your requirements, to send me some, or all, of the note. This, however, is a matter too remote to take steps for yet.

The doctor has been examining my damaged foot and pronounces it to have been a fracture of the ankle bone, in addition the muscular sprain there may have been. It is not yet recovered, but gives me less trouble of late.

Convey my very best remembrances to Mr. Darragh, Rudolf, Richard Brink, and O'Flaherty.

With my very best love to yourself,
I remain, my dear Mother,
Ever your affectionate son,
REG.

Off to Ceylon

What wide-hearted greetings! No gall or bitterness in his loving nature! No narrowness in his large soul.

Mr. Darragh, the strongly loyal priest of St. Mary's, and O'Flaherty, former editor of the "Leader," share his kindly remembrances with Rudolf Meyer, the little fugitive German, whom he picked up in the desert, and Richard Brink, late second Speurder and surrendered burgher.

Dyatalawa, Ceylon,
11th Aug., 1900.

My dearest Mother,

I wrote you a short letter on the 8th inst., notifying my safe arrival at Colombo. We have since continued our journey inland and are now at our ultimate destination. Colombo we reached at 2 a.m. on the 8th, Wednesday.

The sight of land in our immediate vicinity at early dawn was very pleasant after being so long at sea. The surroundings as seen from the ship presented little of interest uncommon to most dockyards, and the heat was intense. But the novelty of other surroundings than those of endless waters enabled us to pass the day pleasantly. During the course of the afternoon a crowd of mixed humanity turned out in boats and rowed round the ships to look its fill. It appears that strange weird stories had preceded us, in which we were set forth as being a fierce crowd of selected desperadoes, culled from the four winds. Some miserable local quill driver had enlarged upon the opportunity to serve up to the public two columns of blood-chilling phantasy and shatter its nerves. I was unaware of this when the sightseers came around, and was, together with my companions, lounging on deck smoking my pipe, and regarding all mankind with constitutional affability. Had I, however, known that something was expected of us, I would have arranged to cork my eyebrows, turn my coat inside out, and eat raw meat upon some suitable eminence.

The next morning at 4.30 we landed and marched between two lines of escort to the train, by which we travelled in nice, roomy carriages, to this place. This first glimpse of the Orient was refreshing, though by no means surprising, nor was there in it anything unexpected. The scope of my experience hitherto is limited to Europe and South Africa; but one is sufficiently acquainted, through literature and otherwise, with the East to know what to expect.

The first part of our journey lay through flat country, amongst vast stretches of swamps, woods, and cultivated fields. Later on the country became more hilly, but still thickly wooded and richly cultivated. Finally we entered the mountains.

To endeavour to present you with a description of the unsurpassed beauty of the scenery would be futile. The train wound up along the face of the mountains, through tunnels, along

Off to Ceylon

crags, and on trestle bridges, over mountain torrents, dashing like a broad stream of white flakes for thousands of feet down the almost precipitous kloofs, till the senses positively swam with intoxication from the rapid succession of varying, indescribable panorama.

I have never seen such a richly watered territory. Every kloof contains a dashing torrent, every declivity is threaded with rills, every valley is the bed of a grand river rolling its turbid waters to the sea. All down the valleys and on the lower slopes are miles upon miles of terraced ricefields. The higher slopes are either laid out in endless tea plantations, or covered with dense forest.

Our camp is about one hundred and twenty miles inland, at an altitude of between four and five thousand feet. It is situated upon the lower hills, within a huge circle of high and beautiful mountains. The climate is fresh and mild, not unlike that of Johannesburg during the December rains. It is, moreover, said to be very healthy. We are well housed and amply fed, and shall, I understand, later on enjoy greater freedom than is afforded by the limits of our fence.

A hundred times I have regretted not bringing with me my Zulu books, as I have much time upon my hands and could get through a deal of study. I think of writing to Durban to order a set and also of buying a few law books at Colombo.

There are none of our old Ladybrand boys

here yet, though probably they will come in time; nor are there any of your acquaintances from Johannesburg among us.

With very best love, believe me, my dear Mother,

Ever your affectionate son,
REG.

Dyatalawa Camp, Ceylon,
18th Aug., 1900.

My dear Sisters,

After many days I am once more enabled to favour myself by writing you a brief communication.

The mortal coil, which more than once of late I have come near shuffling off, still adheres to me in all its entirety. A broken ankle, and a few particles of bombshell embedded in my face and hands, remain as sole record of how near we came to parting. I would gladly have shown more scars in my country's cause, but that privilege is denied me by reason of captivity.

On June 18th last—exactly two months to-day—I was made a prisoner of war at Pretoria. It so happened that on June 4th Roberts made his great attack on Pretoria. The music began about 8.30 a.m., and from start to finish I was in it.

General de la Rey ordered me, with seventeen men, to hold an outpost while the guns and burghers took up their positions behind, in the kopjes. This I did, and having driven in the

Off to Ceylon

advance guard of the enemy, retired, according to orders, upon our main body. There I was assigned a position with my men upon the crest of a rand. The enemy immediately began to pound us with artillery, till we did not know our heels from our heads. It got desperately hot and we had no cover. The fighting line was about six miles broad; so I speak of our position only. We had now about one hundred and fifty men in our kopje, of whom I commanded a small portion. As the day wore on, and as bomb and shrapnel literally swept the ground, we lay on for hour after hour, without the enemy coming within range of our mausers, the men began to give way by twos and threes, until at last there was only six of us left, four officers and two burghers.

We crawled into the best shelter we could get and smoked our pipes, waiting for the charge, which we knew must come before the day was over. We had not eaten since the previous night, and one of the men had taken to his heels with my water can. I sent three different men back to fetch biltong from my saddlebag, but they ate the biltong themselves and did not return.

In my commando I had a mild German, who invariably fell off his horse three times whenever he went out scouting. He wore "giglamp" spectacles, no shirt, a khaki suit tied on with riempjes, the rents in which were repaired by tying them up, like the mouth of a sack. He was the last and only one of my troop remaining with me. I told him to run away too with the rest, as one man more or less made no odds. He said "Nein! fluchten ist gemein!" He was quite happy, he had only one death to die; and the intense sense of relief experienced after the bursting of each bomb, and before the arrival of the next, realized his philosophic ideal of complete happiness in the passing moment. A pipe of tobacco would raise that happiness to the pitch of serenity. He filled a short black pipe, put it upside down in his mouth, and sat nursing his knees. When the shrapnel bullets fell extra thick around him, he just pulled down the brim of his hat and remarked: "Wie gut ist es zu erfahren, dass man noch nicht getroffen wird und ganz ruhig sein kann bis zum nächsten schutz!"

I was trying to persuade myself that I, too, was not afraid; that it was the heat of the sun which made my mouth dry; but I knew all along that, in truth, I was the most frightened man on that hill, and was only restrained by shame from putting my length of leg to good advantage.

We lay there until three o'clock in the afternoon, when the cannonading slackened for a bit. We knew that meant the general attack was coming. Simultaneously we saw a long line of men spreading out across the veldt behind the bult opposite us. I sent my German to go and call up some of our burghers who had taken shelter among the rocks behind us, at the foot of the hill. He returned with twelve.

Off to Ceylon

There we lay, fourteen all told, every man behind his stone, with his mauser charged and cartridge belts loosened for action. Away across the veldt, upon the crest of the bult parallel to us, at two thousand yards, emerged a long line of infantry, about six hundred strong. Behind them, on a higher ridge, stood three fifteen pounders—silent as yet—and, between the infantry and the guns, a dark line of cavalry, about three hundred strong. Those guns will start blowing our heads off, so that we can't raise a finger against the infantry until they are within three hundred yards. Then they will dash at us—six hundred to fourteen—and after them the "vervloekste" lancer, with his dangerous toy, ten foot long, tipped with steel.

It was a gruesome moment. In the silence reigning on both sides the long line of khaki swept towards us. Every man's breath stood still in that awful moment of tension. We have been pounded all day long, unable to fire a shot in return, and now half an hour—nay, ten minutes—will decide our fate. Kingdom come, or not. Bang! on my left. Some man's nerves are overstrung, and he has fired before the time.

"Stilte daar! Wat maak julle!"

"Ik schiet de vervloekste Engelse! Daarom is ik hier!"

"Hou stil! Domkop! Not a shot till they are within twelve hundred yards."

"Stadig, kerels! Laat hulle kry, toen hulle by daar die meershoep kom!"

A few more moments of breathless silence.

"Now then—laat los!"

"R-r-r-r-r-r!"

The advancing line stops, falls flat, and returns the fire.

"R-r-r-r-r-r! Boom! Boom! Boom!"

Maxims, small arms, and cannon play upon us, and the whole pandemonium begins. All nervousness is gone and one is seized with wild intoxication.

"Toe, nou, kerels! Skiet! Skiet! Skiet!"

The roar is so incessant, and the nerves so deadened, that one cannot distinguish the sound of one explosion from another; yet the bombs are bursting over and among us all the time.

Every now and then, as one lies flat and shoots, one feels a concussion from above, which bumps one's face upon the ground, pretty much like a kitten being patted by a small boy. All at once the earth is rent asunder and goes up in flame. As I sprawl across the ground several yards away I dimly hear a shout.

"Allemachtig! Veldcornet is dood! Veldcornet is dood!"

"Nee, hy staat weer op."

That shell struck the rock behind which I was lying. As I got up spluttering and rubbed the dust and splinters out of my beard I realized that the stone had saved me from being blown to atoms.

That line across the veldt was beginning to waver; every man's teeth were set.

A burgher, quite a lad, jumped out of our line and ran like a hare down the hill.

"Shoot him! Shoot him!" was the cry, "let's all die together!"

"Nee, laat hem maar gaan! Hy is maar een kind!"

More cannon had now been turned on us, and I had to bawl orders to the next man.

Once more I was lifted, more violently than before, and "chucked" sprawling on my face. I lay half conscious, choked and blinded, just waiting for the next thing to happen. And the "next thing" came in the shape of a flying lump of stone "whack" on the back of my head. I lay quite still a few seconds longer and just put up my hand to feel where my head was, and get used to things.

"Machtig," said an old gentleman on my right, "Veldcornet's dead right enough this time. The Rondgaande Hof won't see *him* again!"

I distinctly recollect at this moment wondering how you were. I got up, crawled into shelter again and lay there. As I raised my gun to fire, the whole veldt rocked and swayed like the waves of the sea. Every nerve in my body was shattered, and I felt an irresistible impulse to hide my head and let things take their course. In those few moments I felt undiluted "funks." There was the enemy, however, and he had to be driven back. In three quarters of an hour the sun would set and firing would cease. Every man seemed to be fighting against time. A few minutes more and the line of khaki turned and retired back over the bult.

We had hardly time to shout "Hurrah!" before they turned four more cannon on us. They were too far off for us to pick off the gunners, so we had just to lie down flat, with the shells playing the devil's tattoo over us.

The sun was within twenty minutes of setting when we perceived the enemy's cavalry sweeping round our right, behind us, to cut us off from Pretoria. They had taken all our positions on the right. Our kopje was the only one we still held. In a few minutes we should be surrounded, cut off, and killed or captured, all to no purpose. Seeing this we decided to retire, jumping one by one out of the schans and running down the hill to our horses. I was the last to run out. As I dashed down a steep, stony bit, upon which the enemy's maxim was playing, I missed my footing, fell, and incurred a compound sprain, and, as afterwards appeared, a fracture of a small bone.

Somehow I scrambled to the bottom, where I found Mother's little pet pony waiting for me. He took me into town, where I rode to Stockenström's house, and off-saddled to get a few hours' rest and food for pony and myself prior to pushing on to General Botha's commando.

This was the end of my campaigning. I found I was hopelessly disabled, and could not rise to my feet without help. Next morning the khakis

Off to Ceylon

entered the town whilst I was lying at Styx's house, using fearful language. I remained there a fortnight, most carefully tended by my kind host and hostess, till one day, when I was just able to begin getting about, an officer came along, made me a prisoner of war, and sent me, between fixed bayonets, limping to the Provost Marshal. This official let me out on parole to go to Johannesburg and there report myself to his colleague.

I reached Johannesburg in due course and reported myself. Two days later I was cast into the show ground among some two hundred other prisoners of war. Many prisoners taken at that time were liberated on parole, but in my case it was not granted. Among the English and British Afrikanders I am known as "the notorious," on account of the prominent share I took in the invasion of the Western Province (Prieska). Among my own people, on the other hand, I am, for these same reasons, accorded much merit.

The British military authorities had, I am told, at one time intended trying me by court martial on the supposition that I was a British subject; but on ascertaining that I was neither an Englishman nor a British subject, the idea was very justly dropped and I was accorded the treatment of a prisoner of war.

Mr. Darragh and our old friends the Bishop of Mashonaland and Mr. Lyttelton took a deal of trouble in getting the matter rightly represented to Lord Roberts. The treatment I have received from British officers since my capture has been uniformly courteous and honourable.

For ten days I was kept in the Johannesburg show grounds, after which I was sent to Capetown and put into the O.F.S. prisoners' camp at Green Point, where about fifteen hundred men were confined. I fell in there with a lot of my old Magersfontein friends. Frikkie and Johannes v. Reenen, both taken at Paardeberg. Frikkie had a hole through his leg and one through his back, but is now recovered. They both distinguished themselves greatly during the war. Coleman, too, was there; he was Veldcornet of Bloemfontein, and fought with great bravery in fourteen battles. He, too, was wounded and taken when de Villebois fell. v. d. Watt, taken at Paardeberg; S. Ferreira, wounded in the leg. Natie Ferreira has fought more battles than any man in the legal profession. He is secretary to General de la Rey and aide-de-camp. I last saw him in the early part of the battle in which I got disabled. Hans Boshoff and his son are at Green Point too, taken at Paardeberg. Van Rooyen of Moketsi, and several more are there too, Paardeberg prisoners. Poor Hans v. Rooyen was killed at Paardeberg. He had grown to be a remarkably nice young man, honourable, gentlemanly, and brave—that's why he got killed. Harry Stuart is there too. Japie de Villiers is still among that brave remnant with de Wet, to be with whom I would give all I possess. Frans Jacobsz is still at the front with General Botha.

After about a fortnight at Green Point I was marched, with about two hundred and fifty more, on board a steamer, where we ascertained our destination to be Ceylon. We called at Durban, and from there struck across to Colombo, which we reached in about three weeks. At Colombo we were taken ashore and marched to the train which conveyed us hither.

The journey up by rail was through a country of most surpassing beauty, winding along up the mountain sides, each curve of the track disclosing some new and surprising panorama of mountain, wood, and water.

Our camp lies upon the lower hills—a country very much like that of the city of Durham—in a great basin between the mountains. We are well lodged and fed. In common with the other officers I enjoy special advantages. We are supplied with material for cricket and football, and obtain special leave to go out to the field for play. Around the camp is a trench, six miles in circumference, and the officers are allowed out on parole from 10 a.m. to 7 p.m. daily to ramble within the limits of the trench. I went out yesterday and discovered numerous little valleys and woods and streams, where one can pass a pleasant hour. Colonel Vincent and Lieutenant-Colonel Coope are the officers in charge, and do everything in their power to make us happy. Colonel Vincent bears a strong resemblance to Charlie's uncle, old Captain Vincent, though he is much younger, and I cannot but think he is of the same family.

The length of our period of residence here is uncertain, and must necessarily depend upon the duration of the war. The forensic art will, I fear, be a lost art to me by the time I get back, for I have lived for six months in a state of primitive nature in the field. Altogether it is just twelve months since I appeared in a court of law. Nor do I greatly care. The campaign, with its outdoor life, has shaken all the settled instincts of eleven years of city life, and roused my old rural proclivities. Moreover, I have no ties in private life, being as cork, floating on the water. If we lose the country there will be no more public life for me either, unless it be that of the " Opposition Member."

If you were to see me now I think you would fail to recognize the smooth-shaven young barrister to whom you said good-bye on Waterloo platform on the 29th October, 1894. Had you met me on the day I emerged from the Kalahari Desert on April 18th, 1900, after my twelve hundred miles ride, you would still less have known me. Top boots and spurs, in which I had lived and slept for four months; verweel rybrook of equal antiquity and wear; corduroy coat and waistcoat; a hat in which I invariably slept; two bandoliers of cartridges; a mauser and a revolver slung around my body; and a beard and hair which hid my ears and face!

Off to Ceylon

I sat upon a raw-boned, shaggy horse (but worth its weight in gold!), with a blanket behind and a mackintosh in front; upon the saddle a pair of holsters at my knees and a pair of saddlebags at the animal's ribs. No wonder the Kafirs called me "Ou Sieur" and the burghers said "Oom," or "Ou Oom," in addressing me, regardless of the fact that I was frequently the junior of the speaker!

When I think of it it's just like a smell of whisky to an inebriate! The English might have fought till they were blue in the face before I would have laid down my arms, if they had not, in consequence of my accident, captured me.

My ride, to which I refer above, is also probably of interest to you, so I'll tell you about it. You may recollect my having written to you from Kenhardt in the Cape Colony, during the war, about March 10th. I was then serving in the expeditionary force known as the "Prieska Expedition." I had been lying a month in the trenches at Magersfontein, and was getting pretty tired of the inaction it entailed.

When, therefore, at the end of January our old friend, the late Commandant-General Ferreira ordered me to saddle my horse and go along with the Prieska Expedition, I was more than pleased. We left Magersfontein about January 27th, and travelled south-west down to Modder and Vaal rivers. Our force was one hundred and seventy-five men strong, with two guns. On the road we came upon the spoor of the enemy, but were never near enough to do any fighting. On February 13th, at 3 a.m., we reached the Orange River at Zwemkuil, about six hours (thirty-six miles) below the mouth of the Vaal. The Orange River here is about two hundred and fifty to three hundred yards broad, about forty feet deep, and very swift.

The pont had been destroyed, and it was impossible to get over. Our first business was to secure the opposite bank and cut off the line of communication southwards into the Colony. At daybreak a party of burghers stripped and swam across with their guns and ammunition belts laid upon a rough raft. I had the honour to be one of these pioneers. I couldn't swim more than just enough to swear by; but then most of us were in the same condition, and *somebody* had to make a start and set the ball a-rolling. So I volunteered, and just caught on to a trailing rope behind the raft.

Once in possession of both banks we had to get the wagons, horses, cattle, and guns across. For three days we worked like Trojans, with no other mechanical appliances than those we were born with. All that time I went about in Nature's bathing suit, and lived as much in the water as out, sometimes swimming out to mid-stream on a log, heading a troop of horses, or guiding raft-loads of goods. More than once I was from one to two hours up to the armpits working in the water. Finally, we not only got

Off to Ceylon

across our whole commando, but had established a workable pont.

At sunset on February 15th the Hoofd Commandant started for Prieska, which was thirty-six miles distant. He took with him a small body of thirty men, among whom was myself, now promoted from the ranks to his personal staff. I was up to then, and for some time afterwards, only a "general burgher." It was not till some months later that I was elected to a command, since which I have at different times been both a Veldcornet and a Commandant.

We reached Prieska at 4.30 a.m. on February the 16th, took possession of the town before anybody was up or even aware of our approach, and the Commandant read the proclamation annexing Prieska to the Orange Free State the same morning.

The main body came up with us a few days later and proceeded about ten hours (sixty miles) further into the colony to a place called Houtwater, between Prieska and de Aar. I did not accompany them but remained in Prieska, having had certain duties assigned me there by the chief.

On March the 5th I went to the camp at Houtwater, and on the morning of the 6th was present at the battle there when our little force attacked and defeated five companies of the C.I.V. with six guns. I did not get a chance to take part in the fight as the General sent me early in the day to carry a despatch.

On March the 8th I left Prieska along with

the chief and went to Kenhardt, which is situated ninety-six miles due west. The country all about here was hot, dry, and desolate. The sun was like a blazing fire overhead, the roads heavy, and water rare. One frequently had to travel ten, fifteen, or even thirty miles without a drop to drink; even when found it was brackish stuff which had to be hoisted up out of deep wells. On one occasion it was so salty as to make us all sick. On another, after riding eight or nine miles thirsty, we came to a puddle of standing water in the road which had been caught up from a recent shower. We off-saddled and the horses ran to get a drink. There were the bones of a long since dead sheep lying in the water. Then one of the horses lay down and rolled in it! As he did so someone shouted, "Run, run quickly, and fill the water cans from the further edge, before the stirred-up mud gets to it!"

This was done. The water was, nevertheless, of the colour and consistence of thick cocoa. As we drank it we realized that we were swallowing heaps of tadpoles. We were, however, so glad to get the water that nobody hesitated a moment but went on drinking. I am sure my tadpoles did not die quickly, for I felt them wriggling inside me still at night when I went to bed in the veld.

On March the 10th we reached Kenhardt, where we remained till the 14th or 15th. What we did there is immaterial to the present his-

Off to Ceylon

tory; and for reasons, public and private, will not be here recorded. On Friday evening, March the 16th, we reached Upington, on the north bank of the Orange River, eighty miles due north of Kenhardt. A reference to the map will show you that we were by this time nearly two-thirds of the way across the continent.

On Monday, March 18th, in consequence of important news received, it was decided to send me back to Prieska. The distance was one hundred and seventy miles (or twenty-four hours te paard). At sunset on Monday, March 18th, I set out alone with two good horses and a despatch in my pocket. I rode all night and next day at a good stiff canter, just giving the horses a short rest and feed when I came to water. At sunset on Tuesday, as I approached Prieska, I met two men who brought me the information that our commando had retreated to Prieska and crossed the river back into Griqualand, and were in full retreat towards Kimberley. Lord Kitchener, with fifteen hundred men, was in possession of the town and pont at Prieska.

My course had been along the southern bank all the way from Upington. The Prieska pont being in possession of the enemy, it was impossible for me to get across and rejoin our forces on the northern bank without returning all the way to Upington, whence I had come, for the river is deep, swift, and impassable all along here. The English were, moreover, I was informed, coming down the road towards me with the object of reaching Kenhardt, and subsequently Upington.

I sat down on the road and ate some biltong and drank muddy water, whilst I took bitter counsel with myself. Finally, the council decided to turn and fall back on Kenhardt (sixty miles off) with the whole detachment of one man. Previous to doing so, however, the whole force lay down and slept for two hours. Rising with the moon I pushed on steadily. The open sea is often spoken of as conveying a sense of solitude and isolation, but I assure you the sound of the gentlest rippling wave is tumult compared with the solitude of those vast plains at night. Hour after hour, mile after mile, I pushed on, the whole expanse as flat as a billiard table and thickly covered with short, stiff, scrubby bush, which would not quiver in the strongest hurricane. Not a mountain, not a kopje, not even a bult to vary the dead flatness. Not a house to be seen or encountered for thirty miles, and not a sound all the way but the rhythmical clatter of the horse's hoofs and the jingle of the mauser carbine. The stars rose and set again, but I kept steadily on my way, with nothing but my own thoughts for company.

At one p.m. on Wednesday the 21st I reached Kenhardt, where I found everything gone wrong, and, instead of a strong commando, nothing but a few fugitives.

From Upington I received news that the

Off to Ceylon

chief and his staff had cut their cables and made a bee-line along the north bank of the river to join our retreating commando. I was in a nice hole. In the last forty-two hours I had ridden *one hundred and sixty-eight miles* and enjoyed *four hours'* sleep. I was seven hundred miles from Pretoria, and two hundred from my own commando with an English force between it and me. On the north was the impassable river and the intraversable Kalahari desert, while to the west I had free scope to travel two hundred and fifty miles, until I arrived at the sea coast—and more British garrisons. My horses were exhausted, and in my pocket I had just four pounds. My mauser was still true, but General Kitchener had fifteen hundred just as good. In addition I had a rope round my neck, it being at that time believed by the English commanders down there that I was English born and a British subject.

The forces at Kenhardt, all colonial, were too disorganized to rally, and everybody was making the best of his way home. That evening there turned up three more Transvaal burghers, who had also been out on remote outpost duty. We decided to make a dash together for home.

Selecting two of our best wagons, a span of mules and another of oxen, we loaded the wagons with ammunition and provisions. About twenty young men of those parts, who had previously joined our commandos and who were anxious to escape to the Transvaal, joined our party. That same night I sent out the whole party, with instructions to take the north road and make for Upington. I myself remained behind to settle a few matters in Kenhardt and do the rearguard scouting in case the enemy should approach.

The next day, Thursday the 22nd, at about 3 p.m., I took my own horse and rode out south along the Carnarvon road. Before I had gone far I came upon the khakis right enough. At about two thousand yards distance a patrol of some fifteen were approaching. Turning my horse's head, I rode into town, locked up the public offices, and after giving the keys to a local resident—there were no *men* left, only women—I rode out of the town on one side, while the khakis came in on the other.

That evening at dark I caught up with my party about fifteen miles away. I sent on the wagons and most of the men, myself and five others remaining behind, nicely entrenched in a sand-hill, to parley with anybody who should come up from behind.

I was just about tired out at this stage. This was the identical spot upon which I had slept that night week. Since that date I had ridden three hundred miles in all, and for the last three nights I had slept just two hours each night. Besides which I was undergoing the mental exhaustion arising from the realization of our first great reverse at Paardeberg (news

Off to Ceylon

of which had reached us) with all its concomitant effects.

After placing the sentries I turned in and slept like a steam engine. But such was the excited state of my mind that, the men told me, I kept getting up in my sleep, giving orders and talking.

Before daybreak we started again. At noon we were overtaken by a tropical storm, and the rain continued for the next four days. At dark the following day, Saturday 24th, we crossed the river and entered the town of Upington wet and tired, but of good cheer.

This rain was our salvation, for not only did it prevent the enemy who, two hundred strong, were on our heels from catching up with us, but also, some days later, we were saved from death by thirst while crossing the desert through the discovery of some rain water, caught in holes on the face of a rock.

Our cattle and horses were now weary and footsore, and the rain was still descending in torrents, so we decided to give them a rest. Our little force, which varied from day to day, now numbered about twenty, while, according to the advices of our scouts the enemy, several hundred strong with cannon, was advancing upon us, but was at that moment stuck in the muddy roads.

Our position was pretty "tight" at this juncture. We were camped on the north bank of the river, on the outer bend of a vast elbow.

North of us lay about a thousand miles of the Kalahari Desert. To the west two hundred miles of Kalahari would bring us to German territory. Six or seven hundred miles to the north-east lay Pretoria. The first hundred and twenty miles of the direct road to Pretoria lay through a narrow strip of the Kalahari which, however, could be avoided by travelling in a south-easterly direction along the north bank of the elbow of the river, entailing a detour of two hundred miles. We decided to take this road.

Accordingly on Tuesday, March 27th, I sent on the wagons and some of the men, myself remaining behind with nine men to guard the pont in case the enemy should come up too rapidly on our rear. The khakis had probably anticipated that we should take this road, for shortly after the wagons had started I received news that they had sent a force across country to cross the river and cut us off about eighty miles higher up. Had we continued our journey on this road we should have found ourselves with an intercepting force in front, a pursuing force behind, the intraversable desert on our left, and the impassable river on our right. You must recollect that, under the existing conditions, we could not afford to risk unnecessary fighting, for we were twenty strong and without cannon, while our pursuers were about seventeen hundred, with whole batteries of artillery.

Off to Ceylon

We had, therefore, only one course left. That was to strike off to the left (N.E.) along a narrow track across the Kalahari, and take our chance. This was no small undertaking, as you will learn from the sequel.

On Thursday, March 29th, I received word that the wagons had got to a reasonably safe point. So we saddled up and followed them. At sunset we rode out of Upington, and at sunrise next morning Colonel Hughes, with his advance guard, entered it. I caught up to the wagons that morning and spent the rest of the day at the outspan, the sun being too hot to allow us to travel. We were on the edge of the desert—which begins as suddenly as the sand on the beach, and is a good bit worse—beside a pool of water. We had before us a stretch of ninety to one hundred miles absolutely without water. That does not mean that there was a lack of *good* water, or of a sufficiency of water; it means that for the whole distance the road lay across one vast plain of deep, soft, yellow sand—*and nothing else*—into which the animals' hoofs sank six inches at each step as they staggered along, with tongues hanging out and eyes rolling, dragging after them the wagons, the wheels of which sank in so deep that the axles often scraped the ground.

To one on foot walking was most painful. At each step the shifting sand gave way under the tread, whilst the blazing sun beat down from overhead, till a man's heart broke from utter weariness and he threw himself down, crying out for death as a relief.

At intervals, stretching across the path, were long, steep ridges, sand-dunes—for all the world like great earthworks—three, five, six, ten, and even twelve, all running in parallel lines. These had to be scaled in succesion, at the cost of infinite shouting, sweating, and panting. Add to this the fact that along the whole road not only is there no river, pool, or spring, nor any drop of water, but also the deepest borings have failed to discover any— and you have the Kalahari grass and bush, strange to say, there in plenty.

On the evening of Friday, March 30th, at sunset every man filled his waterbag and drank all he could hold, and we set off into that desert in earnest. We met a Kafir who told us that rain had fallen in the interior, and that upon the surface of a certain flat rock, at a certain spot fifty miles ahead, we should find a pool of water, unless it had since dried up.

Three men were sent on ahead on good horses to discover this treasure and bring us word—a task little less difficult than searching for "Mercutio's reasons."

All that night we trekked and all next day. Our small supply of water was exhausted in the fatigues of the first few hours. Towards midday we began to suffer severely; as the afternoon wore on it got to be almost more than man or beast could support. We were, however, buoyed up by the hope that our men would return with the news of water. But time went by and there were no signs of them. Despair seized hold of us. The sun was nearly setting. We had been twenty-four hours without water in that fierce heat, where an hour occasions more thirst than twelve under ordinary circumstances. There was not a man or beast among us who was fit to do another two miles. We just looked at each other and came to the conclusion the game was up.

Sighed one big German of our band: "Ja! das Spiel ist aus!"

Personally I felt like a wild beast. Just as the last rays of the sun were tipping the bushes I turned fiercely upon my nearest companion and told him that if I *had* to die I'd do it at my ease lying down, and not undergo the agony of more walking through that awful sand. This seemed to meet the general view, and all voted for off-saddling. I rose and took one last look around the plain.

As I did so I caught sight of a man sitting behind a bush about three hundred yards further on. He was one of those sent to seek water. We dragged ourselves to where he sat, and heard from him that there was water a couple of miles away.

The news operated like magic and roused us to fresh and furious efforts upon our jaded animals. When we got there we found a bare, sloping "klip-plaat" rock, with four small pot-holes along its surface, each filled with muddy rain-water.

Springing from the saddle we fell flat on the ground, and every man buried his face in the puddles. The horses, too, made a rush for the water, and with their noses pushed away those of their masters. Man and beast literally fought each other for the first drink.

By eight o'clock every man had had a reasonable quantity and every beast one good drink, though their thirst was not appeased by a long way. We had stored up exactly one gill of water per man for the next morning, and after that every drop of water upon the rock was exhausted. The rock was even *licked dry* by the oxen.

Having appeased our thirst we threw ourselves upon the ground and smoked a pipe. We were too tired to eat, but the release from that fearful thirst and the delicious, fragrant coolness of the desert by night was positive happiness.

After half an hour's rest I called together the Krijgs Raad (Council of War); for to-morrow morning the sun would come up again, with all its fierce, blazing heat, and we should re-enact to-day's *rôle* with all its horror.

Our situation was by no means an enviable one. True, we no longer had any fear of pursuit by the enemy. The very idea of those poor Tommies, in their "onnozelheid," performing the journey we had that day done was out of the question. *Our* danger lay in the situation. The water was done, and so were our animals. We must quit this spot as soon as it was day. To remain there was certain death. There was only one road, and that was straight ahead. The nearest water was fifty miles off. Neither we nor our animals could reach that, even though we left the wagons to their fate, and pushed on with all the men mounted on their strongest horses. Somebody said he knew of water *thirty* miles away, at right angles to our course. We could reach it across country by abandoning the wagons. That water would last us two days, and then we should have to go seventy miles to the next water. Another man spoke up and said he knew of a place *twenty* miles away where water was usually to be found, but he could not say if there was any now. If we found water there we could exist for a fortnight. If not, we should eventually die.

These proposals were too much fraught with uncertainty and danger to leave us anything but Hobson's choice as to pushing on in the direct road. Even that was much like suicide.

Finally, there up and spoke a little German. He said he had once been lost somewhere in these parts and had, after many wanderings, come upon a little pool of water at the foot of a kopje. This afternoon he had noticed ahead of us, about twenty miles, a kopje which looked like the same, although he could not say for certain.

I've looked death in the face many times this last twelvemonth, but I think he never grinned so exasperatingly as on that night. The seaman upon a raft in mid-ocean is not more powerless than the traveller lost in the Kalahari. The seaman can at least slip off his plank and drown quickly. It is more difficult to drown in a sea of sand!

The off chance of the kopje and the pool decided us, and it was agreed to push on straight ahead. We slept, and rose early next morning. Having eaten a morsel, each man drank the gill of water doled out to him. One poor chap spilt his. In ten minutes we were again as thirsty as ever. You, as a physician, will know that a thirst such as ours, which cracks the lips and parches every nerve in the body, is not allayed by one draught of water.

We hunted among the rocks for zuring (sorrel), which we chewed for the rest of the day. I picked and ate some wild cucumbers, which took the skin off my mouth and throat for a whole week. Men were sent on ahead to look for the kopje and the pool. When, or if, found, a revolver was to be fired to announce the glad tidings. And so we plodded on through the sand.

Needless to go into the details of this second day. Suffice it to say at sunset I met one of the men returning with a horse loaded with water-

Off to Ceylon

bags; and we drank and drank and drank until the steam hissed out of our red-hot throats. At ten o'clock p.m. we reached the water. It was just a little pool, about as big as the fountain you know so well at Zonnebloem. But it saved us.

Before going to sleep I absorbed about a gallon of water, and laid a bagful at my head against the saddle, and whenever I woke in the night I took a pull. This water lasted us thirty-six hours, allowing during that period one drink for each ox, two for each horse and mule, and unlimited for each man. For the whole of that time we just lay around under the bushes, drinking water, eating a little, and for the rest smoking and sleeping. I personally felt as if I had been sjambokked all over and hung out to stiffen.

This was the end of our troubles. When next we inspanned our beasts were well rested. One smart trek, from sunset to daybreak, brought us out of the desert to a place in the Langeberg Range, where we had grass and water in plenty, and where we took a week's rest.

We were here joined by more fugitives, and had quite a nice little commando together. A unanimous election made me Commandant, and we were ready for further operations. The place where our laager then stood was about ninety hours (five hundred and forty miles) from Pretoria. We were quite in the dark about what our armies had been doing during the last month, so, at the express demand of my own and some neighbouring commandos, I proceeded up country to the Transvaal, where I was to perform—and did perform—certain matters which I am not at liberty to relate here. Let me chronicle in passing that I never again saw that brave little band. On my way back from Pretoria to rejoin them, the English broke through the Vaal at Fourteen Streams, and I was driven back eastwards, with our western army, upon Pretoria; while my lads, after fighting splendidly for some time, losing in battle my temporary successor, were broken up, killed, captured, or driven back into the desert, as their individual fortune befell.

Had I been able to foresee these events I should never have left them, and the history of one section, at least, of this war might have been very different.

To return. After a ride of one thousand miles I reached General Du Toit's camp at Fourteen Streams on April 16th, and then, for the first time for two months, was able to communicate direct with home. Mother, who for six weeks had been under the impression that I was a prisoner, when she received my wire, instead of being glad about my liberty, wanted to faint.

She thought that being prisoner of war was all jam and skittles; that the good, kind English would be *so* nice and pleasant to me!

When, however, I was really taken, and she

found that some of my old Johannesburg acquaintances in the I.L.H. wanted the English to court-martial and shoot me, she changed her mind. I may, however, here add that the counsels of my bloodthirsty friends were not followed, and that I am now very comfortable.

Sept. 20th.

I have been many days writing this letter, as shown by the many kinds of pen, paper, and ink used upon it. I have been all the time praying for the soul of the unfortunate censor who will have to read it over. He will undoubtedly attain perdition in the achievement, unless he be a man not given to swearing.

I have often wondered how you have managed to get along all this time without money from home. I understand you have passed your intermediate M.B. in the interval. Permit me to offer you my congratulations. How far does that enable you to exercise your profession? My reason for asking is a substantial one. It would be advisable if you can now take M.R.C.S. to do so, and not to wait for M.B. before obtaining the technical qualification. It is possible we may find ourselves undischarged bankrupts before this war is over. If we succeed in retaining the Independence—which is even yet not out of the question—I shall retain my profession and position in the State. Should, however, the English succeed in annexing the country, not only my position is gone, but most probably my occupation as a member of the Bar.

I do not yet know what I shall do. Perhaps California may be my next home, perhaps Madagascar, perhaps the Transvaal. But in any case I expect that for some years to come I shall have to live by turning my hand to whatever comes in my way. Certain it is that the channel of my future career will be directed more by political than by private considerations.

In all my calculations, until this war broke out, I have been influenced by the consideration of, in the best manner possible, fulfilling my duty as a son, and having due regard to my obligations to Mother. Now, however, I shall be influenced at all times first by my duty to my country. Should that duty preclude me from doing the best possible for myself and mine, I shall not hesitate to let my own interests suffer. It may, consequently, devolve upon you to look after Mother. I do not know to what extent she has suffered financial loss by the troubles. That we shall only ascertain after it is all over. For months, however, Senekal has been one of the chief bases of operation in the O. F. S., and many and many a house has gone down in ashes in those parts.

Personally I am "broke"—clean. My creditors will be secured and paid in full unless they destroy their own chances; but I myself shall

Off to Ceylon

have about sixpence left. That, however, will not trouble me in the least. I can always get on. But I think you would be just at the right time if you came out to Johannesburg when things are settled. There will inevitably occur one of those big speculative booms, accompanied by a large influx of population, whichever way it ends.

We have now three thousand eight hundred prisoners in our camp. Among those just arrived are Cornelis Ferreira, Schalk and Willem Jacobsz, Georgie Sennett, Hans van Rooyen's three sons, Justus, their cousin, Isaac Jacobsz, J. van Rensburg, and heaps more. Lindeques Bennie and Johnnie Sennett (thirteen and fourteen respectively) were made prisoners on the battlefield, fighting, but were sent home to their mother on parole. Jan Jacobsz (Jan's zoon) and Petrus Ferreira (P.'s zoon) are here too. Pieter Ferreira, Oom Naas's son, is expected with the next batch. Oom Naas and his seven sons have all proved themselves splendid men, superior even to the high estimate we always placed on them. Their courage and resource is proved, whilst their humanity and honour stand equally high.

You can address me when writing, "Veldcornet F. R. Mostyn Cleaver, Transvaal Prisoner of War, Dyatalawa Camp, Ceylon." I shall be pleased to hear from you. Remember me to David and let him see such portions of this letter as are interesting to him. I want you also to send to the Wild Man of California either a copy, or the original, of such of it as is interesting.

With very best love to you both, believe me,
Ever your affectionate brother,
F. R. MOSTYN CLEAVER.

P.S.—I enclose a few cinnamon leaves, picked during my rambles.

Dyatalawa, Ceylon,
Aug. 20th, 1900.

My dear Mother,

I am in receipt of a letter from you, dated July 15th, which has been forwarded from Cape Town. You are, I daresay, by now aware that I was not let out there on parole, but consigned to the prisoners' camp. I never asked for parole, nor was it offered me. I wrote you once or twice from Green Point and also from Durban, which letters you will have received by now.

We are jogging along pretty comfortably. Since last I wrote the authorities have supplied us with cricket and football material and send us out daily in batches to play. In addition, the officers are allowed to ramble daily within a mile and a half radius of the camp in the valleys. This exercise I find most beneficial to both mind and body.

We were very comfortable on board ship, but the hateful odour of sea water and engines

Off to Ceylon

clung about me until I was able to eliminate it by a smell of the veld.

There are three hundred of us at present, but next week we expect another fifteen hundred. We make things as pleasant as possible and pass the time agreeably, building up social interests among ourselves. The Colonel has given us a large recreation and sporting hall. The Germans and Hollanders have their Zangvereine; the Irish have their boxing and athletic exercises; the Afrikanders impartially take part in everything and bake stormjagers en pannekoek in the intervals.

What has become of Sheppard? I feel sufficiently interested in him to wish to know if he has got out of his troubles. Do you know anything of Styx? Correspondence is a difficult matter when life is cast upon such even waters as mine at present, and when the one subject of paramount interest is that of politics which we may not touch upon.

I am keeping in perfect health and good cheer. If I know that you yourself are easy in mind, you will remove my only possible source of unhappiness.

With very best love, believe me, my dearest Mother,

Ever your affectionate son,

REG.

Dyatalawa Camp, Ceylon,
Sept. 5th, 1900.

R. Fenton, Esq.,
  Coronado Beach,
    Cal., U.S.A.

My dear Uncle,

It is so long since I last wrote to you that I can no longer remember when it was. I am at present a prisoner of war in Ceylon. After helping to fight the battles of my country for six months, I broke my ankle in the fight before Pretoria on June the 4th and was unable to follow my comrades in the retreat of our army. I managed that night to escape off the field into the town of Pretoria. The next day the enemy entered and took possession of the capital. I remained quietly at the house of a friend undiscovered. On June the 18th, being so far recovered as to be able to walk about the grounds by the aid of a stick, I got involved in a dispute with some British military officers. One of them asked me, with what looked to my sore feelings like a sneer, "if I had not now had enough of fighting?" I replied, "No; my most ardent desire is to be on the high veld, with my rifle on my back, sharing the fortunes of my fellow burghers."

Thereupon he arrested me and sent me to Major Poore. The sergeant and Tommies under whose charge I limped along the street were as gentle as nurses with me, asking if they went too quickly and assisting me all

Off to Ceylon

they could. Tommy is the best fellow that ever trod upon shoe leather.

To Major Poore I was reported as a dangerous malignant. But when upon questioning me I told him the same as I had done the one who arrested me, he gave it as his opinion that my expressions were those of an honourable man and loyal burgher. He at once gave me my parole, and asked if I desired any other favour.

I told him that my Mother was in Johannesburg, unaware of and sorely anxious as to my fate. He thereupon gave me permission to go to Johannesburg on parole and there report myself. My parole was here re-granted, but after forty-eight hours withdrawn. The exact reason is unknown to me; but probably in consequence of Lord Roberts's proclamation relative to officers who had taken a prominent part in the war.

I was sitting chatting with an officer of the I.L.H. for whom, in pre-war days and still, I entertained a warm regard, when a detachment came to arrest me. Mother had gone to bed. I went to her door and tapped, telling her not to be alarmed, but I was arrested.

Poor Mother! She slipped into her dressing-gown and came downstairs. The guard who stood in the room had been one of my own town police. He looked at Mother quite humbly and somewhat frightened, because Mother can, it is well known, be "kwaai" upon occasion.

"I am very sorry," he said, "to have to

arrest my old baas, but I am forced to do my duty."

I went down with —— to the guard-house and he bailed me out until 9 a.m. the next day (Saturday). At 8.30 a.m. I got into a cab and drove to the Agricultural Show Yard, which was the prisoners' camp. My first reception was somewhat curt. Shortly afterwards there came a change, of which I understood the cause from Mother later on. It was this. When I entered Colonel Wright's presence Willy Begbie was talking to him and came forward and shook hands with me. It seems, after I retired, the Colonel said to Begbie, "Do you know that fellow?"

"Yes, I know him well," was the reply.

"And what kind of man is he?"

"A gentleman in every sense of the word."

"But he is an Englishman!"

"Oh no! I beg your pardon; he is a Free State burgher born and an official of the Transvaal."

"Ah! that makes all the difference."

In the afternoon Mother wrote up to ask permission to visit me. But owing to the escape of a burgher the day previous, all visitors were barred except upon special permit from the military governor. This, through the friendly offices of Mr. Darragh, who guaranteed her loyalty—you know Mother is staunch and even passionate English—was granted and on Tuesday Mother came up.

Off to Ceylon

Colonel Wright treated her quite chivalrously, giving her his own room in which to receive me, and refusing to look into anything she had brought for me, saying he had heard of Mother, and would not think of inspecting what she had brought. She came more than once and I did what I could to comfort her.

On the 30th June came sudden orders that we were all to be sent down to Cape Town, and I telephoned to Mother, who came up at once. But our departure did not take place until Sunday morning the 1st July. Mother alone was permitted to accompany the procession of prisoners to the station. That was the last I saw of her. Poor Mother! Her sorrow is my only trouble.

I remained at the Green Point camp for a fortnight, and then was shipped across to Ceylon with the first batch of prisoners. We have now been here a month.

I cannot here give you a history of my adventures through the war. It would entail more writing than I am prepared to undertake. But I am writing somewhat fuller details to Nancy and will ask her to send on the letter to you when she has done with it.

For the first two months I was " Home Veld-cornet" of Jeppestown, and entrusted with the organization and command of the special police in that district. I had asked leave to go to the front with the very first commandos on Sept. 29th, but this was refused me. In

December, however, I hit upon the subterfuge of " a month's leave to the front," and my chief saw me no more. I joined as an ordinary fighting burgher. Four months later I returned to Johannesburg for a few days, and was pressed to accept the post of chief in my old office. But I flourished at the State Secretary my appointments as Commandant and legal adviser to the General, and returned to the front with laughter in my mouth.

On Dec. the 17th, 1899, I went to Magersfontein, where I spent five or six weeks under General Ferreira. He was our old friend Oom Naas, Commandant of Korannaberg, who had become Commandant-General of the O.V.S. He was subsequently shot dead accidentally by one of his own men, in a night alarm near Kimberley, about Feb. 18th. He was a man in a thousand —almost in a generation—he does not leave his fellow behind him.

Early in February I went down into the Western Province with the Prieska Expedition. We did some grand work there, but had to retreat before Kitchener after Paardeberg. It was during this retreat of our little force that I had the most personally exciting experience of the whole war. I was out riding despatches when the commando withdrew across the Orange River back into Griqualand West, and I got cut off all by my lone self. I had to ride across country from Prieska to Kenhardt, thence to Upington, and from Upington

Off to Ceylon

through the Kalahari Desert into the Langeberg Range. Thence to Fourteen Streams, where I rejoined my commando, after having been reported captured for two months. I had ridden seven hundred and fifty miles, for a good part of which the enemy's scouts had been close at my heels. Once, in fact, when I was quite alone, in the heart of the hostile territory, fifteen scouts hove in sight. I decided " to put my trust in the legs of a horse," and using my spurs, I proved the Psalmist's conclusions to be wrong for once.

I had a raw-boned, flat-chested, red-brown nag, who held his tail sideways, like the disabled rudder of a ship, and clattered his hoofs together when he walked. But he had an eye like a diamond! Whenever anybody saw his tail, they jeered; but when next moment they saw his eye, they fetched out rolls of bank notes and offered fabulous prices for him.

I've never sat across a better beast. He carried me twelve hundred miles without a break on that expedition, and finally fell into the hands of the enemy thus:

On my return to Johannesburg I left him with Mother to rest a little and get fed up. On the 27th May our commandeering officer ordered Mother to give him up, to go to Klip River against Roberts. She stoutly refused, and got an order from van den Berg authorizing her to keep him for my use. But upon the occupation of the town by Lord Roberts, the

British had such sore need of remounts that an order was issued ordering up all horses except those retained by special permit. Mother drove him to the office to ask a permit, and, thinking to make a good case, told how he had carried a heavy man so many hundred miles and therefore must be utterly exhausted. She was told to come again, but as she drove home my poor old friend was seized in the street and all the grace allowed Mother was to drive home. I hope he has broken the neck of the man who took him!

After coming through the desert I returned to Johannesburg for a week's visit and then went back to the front. This was just at the time of Roberts's advance on Kroonstad. I went down to the western frontier, where I was given command of the scouts. I served through the retreat along the Vaal River and in the north of the Orange Free State. I participated in the last stand around Johannesburg, at Langlaagte, and in the retreat on Pretoria.

At Pretoria I fought in the general engagement of June 4th. Although lying for seven hours under severe cannon and rifle fire, and being twice hurled away by the draught of bombs which exploded within four feet of me, I escaped without further injury than having my hands and face full of fine iron splinters.

As the sun was setting and we fled from the field, I had to run down the steep hill-side across a narrow zone of fire. In doing this I fell and broke my ankle. Hinc illae lachrymae! But for

Off to Ceylon

this insignificant incident I should now either have inherited my *seven* foot of earth, or have been still in the fighting line.

We are here very comfortably fixed up. Our camp is situated one hundred and fifty miles from Colombo. We are almost upon the equator; but owing to our being about four thousand feet above the sea level the climate is very pleasant. At present there are about eight hundred of us, but fresh consignments are constantly arriving and the number will shortly be up to four thousand or more.

The camp consists of about eighty huts. Around this there is a double line of barbed wire with sentries. At night the whole fence is brilliantly illuminated by electricity.

The garrison is upon an eminence above close by. Inside our fence there is a store and a recreation room. We have amongst us a couple of world competing athletes, and also men of musical and artistic skill, besides doctors, lawyers, engineers, and a parson; so we constitute a community of an average order.

We are allowed out under escort to play cricket and football daily; so we get good healthy exercise. The officers, of whom I am one, are allowed out every other day on parole, from 10 a.m. to 7 p.m., to ramble about the hills within a radius of about one and a half miles from the camp. There are many little clumps of bush, brooks, and valleys which it is pleasant to explore.

It is impossible to say how long we shall

remain here. In any case for certain until every sign of active war is past. For my own part I find it more soothing to be here, out of sight of the outward and visible signs of the military power now spread over a portion of my native land. If I cannot meet them face to face, with a gun in my hand, I would rather not see them at all.

I read a letter written by you to Mother after the occupation by Lord Roberts. Politics is a subject we are not supposed to say much upon when writing from here, but I will so far transgress the rule as to say that I was *very, very*, sorry to see that you, whom I have always looked upon as a staunch Afrikander, had disappointed me. Maybe it is the result of insufficient data. I laughed sardonically when I read your Utopian picture of an all-round reconciliation after the war, and a pan-Anglican South Africa with the Boers "out-Englishing the English in Imperialism in ten years time!"

You once, in one of your talks, likened us Boers to the elephant. The elephant, I may observe, never forgives. He just waits his opportunity. The O.F.S. and Z.A.R. are annexed, but Steyn, Kruger, De Wet, and Botha are still at large. "First catch your hare, etc." (See Mrs. Beaton, p. 25.)

I wish now to ask you for information. Under certain contingencies I might wish to go over to the States and join you in California. In considering the prospect, I do not necessarily confine myself to the legal profession. In fact, for reasons not needing enumeration here, I doubt whether I shall again exercise it in the Transvaal. I've got very little means of my own. At most I could show a couple of hundreds to the good after paying Aunt Mary the seven or eight hundred pounds I have of hers. I should like to know whether, by combining our energies in running the farm of yours, we could get through life?

Mother was still active and well when last I saw her, though much troubled by the anxieties of the war. I had a letter from her yesterday in which she writes cheerfully.

During the war that ——— became industrious and worked in the mines at a pound a day, to the great improvement of his morals, but at the loss of much rich nasal colouring.

I myself am keeping in good condition, though at first the reaction from outdoor life to the inactivity of tronk told upon me considerably. Now, however, that my leg is recovering and I am able to play a little cricket, I feel better. With love to yourself, Aunt Mary, and Adelaide,

Believe me, your affectionate nephew,

F. R. MOSTYN CLEAVER.

Dyatalawa Camp,
Ceylon, Sept. 10th, 1900.

Mrs. Cleaver,
    J'burg, Z.A.R.
My dearest Mother,

I am in receipt of your letter of July 26th. I am surprised at your not having heard a word from me by then. I expect it is due to our energetic general, de Wet, having interrupted the line of communication. If that be really the cause, I hope you may never receive any of the letters I write. I wrote you from Durban on July 24th and also before that from Green Point.

If you have got any money to spare you can send me a ten pound note. By now you will have received my letter, in which I previously put the same request, of which this is a repetition. After three months you can, if you have it to spare, *but not otherwise*, send me another ten pounds. I have very few expenses here, only a few shillings now and then for tobacco and extras. Ceylon is as big a sell as Max O'Rell's Southern Cross. Everything is as dear and many things dearer than in Johannesburg; consequently I buy nothing but what I require. I shall be glad if Nathan takes the house. I have heard from prisoners, lately arrived, that Cornelis Ferreira is a prisoner of war in Green Point, and that Commandant Pieter and Veldcornet Nikkel (Ferreira) were captured with Prinsloo and will probably be here in a few days' time.

Blaauw (Martinus Lindique), Justus and Groot Naas (v. Rooyens), and three of Hans v. Rooyen's sons will also be here shortly. That surrender of Prinsloo seems to have been brought about by treason on the part of some of the leaders.

The health of the camp is good, and we are all very happy.

Mrs. Bramley's three sons are all prisoners of war. Charley, the youngest, is here. David Grewar, husband of Annie Lindique, of Moketsi is here, and Piet Moketsi is on the road (sea). Bernstein, who used to be with Kuhn in Senekal, and whom you visited in hospital, is here. He was taken in the same engagement in which I was knocked out. He wishes to be remembered to you. He asks you to tell Kuhn.

Let Mrs. Menton know, through Richard Brink, that Menton is exceedingly fit.

With my very best love to you,
    Believe me, my dear Mother,
        Ever your affectionate son,
           F. R. MOSTYN CLEAVER.

P.S.—Five pounds reward for the man in de Wet's commando who captures this letter out of the post before it reaches Johannesburg.
           F. R. M. C.

        Dyatalawa Camp,
           Ceylon, Oct. 3rd, 1900.

David Oliver, Esq.,
    Goldsmith Buildings,
        Temple, London, E.C.

My dear David,

Purely in the spirit of waywardness I take up my pen to write you These Presents. Ofttimes the voice of conscience has smitten me, for that it was many moons before the war that you had written to me and were still unanswered. But the voice of the flesh, being idly disposed, and the hands being of late more familiar with the mauser than with the pen, prevailed. My address, as above, is doubtless unfamiliar to you; but know, O gentle David, that I am travelling in far countries for the good of your country, and the detriment of mine. I am experiencing in practice that, although "stone walls do not a prison make," the reverse is the case with barbed wires and a maxim at every angle! Gladly would I elude the vigilance of the patient sentry and once more stray back to the peaceful occupation of wrecking commissariat trains; only I fear that the disturbance of his philosophic meditations might result in his firing *at me* and *hitting* some peaceful inhabitant of some other part of the camp who wasn't doing anything!

The position, however, has its advantages, for should you to-day wish to interview me, you would have to get a pass, and behind his rampart of ten double-strand barbed wire "X No. —" would laugh to scorn the fierce look with which eleven years ago you terrified him in the Middle Temple Hall! In other words, your humble servant is, at this moment, enjoying that enforced seclusion to which, in the past, he has so frequently, dry-eyed, consigned his fellow men.

Many years ago I once strayed into a chapel in South London and heard the preacher, in realistic terms, describe the scene of the "Good Man" opening the prison doors and leading forth the captive to the banquet.

The indigenous Ceylon buffalo is a harmless, gentle creature, but his flesh is tough and stringy, while toothpicks are scarce; nor does the limited number of geese, slain upon the premises, afford material sufficient for the construction of home-made toothpicks. My thoughts have, in consequence, of late frequently reverted to the preacher's words. I have pictured that "Good Man" in unobtrusive black—swallow tailed and cut away—with a spotless napkin over his arm, entering at the main gate—where those four Khakis grow alongside that wicked hand maxim—bowing and saying, "Soup's served, Sir! This way, Sir! Turtle, Sir?" I have pictured myself in one of the appreciative pauses of soups, leaning over to the "Good Man" saying, "See that you bring me just a nice, crisp bit of venison, put the champagne on ice, and mind you don't bring me *leg* of fowl nor half melted butter with the asparagus!" I have seen myself, half an hour later, critically wiping the dew off the champagne glass and lighting the half-crown Havannah, after drinking to the memory of the whole teams of Ceylon buffalo and South African trek oxen, which I have devoured in the last twelve months; to the hogsheads of slime, tadpoles, and microbes I have swallowed to quench my thirst on dusty marches and to the pounds of black plug and sailor's twist I have stuffed into my pipe on scouting outpost.

This, and much more, I have seen with the mind's eye, but to all these, the eye of the flesh is closed. In vain have I gazed to all points of the horizon, hoping that that "Good Man" may, after all, only have lost his way and be coming. But as I crane over that fence I see nought but the Evil One, dressed in khaki, who stamps the earth with his gun, crying, "'Alt! 'oo goes there? Git off that fence, or d'ye want me to fire one shot 'afore I leave the blooming harmy!"

When I heard that seductive parson it occurred to me that his doctrines were somewhat at variance with Stephen's Criminal Law. Now, however, I am convinced that he was a liar. Stephen has never failed me. To him I trace many a forensic triumph; while the parson, when put to the test, has proved himself a liar, and a fluent liar withal. Almost am I tempted to become a sceptic!

In my short life I have seen many phases of existence, but this present one of prisoner of war is the funniest of them all; that is, provided you look at it in the right light.

Your humble friend laid down his pen just twelve months ago and took up his gun. I carried that gun eight months, and then, owing to the breaking of my right ankle-bone on the field of battle outside Pretoria, on the 4th of June, my gun and I parted company.

Off to Ceylon

In common with the rest of mankind I have had my share of disappointments and griefs; but never has anything affected me so severely as when I had the misfortune to be compelled to retire from the lists of those still actively engaged in the defence of the Vaderland. I have the consolation to have been taken fighting, though I should far rather not have been taken at all. Not that I care one infinitesimal rap for anything that it is possible to incur as a prisoner of war, but the bitterness of having to sit still, impotent, while the very vitals are being trampled out of my country, is positively indescribable. The war, however, is not over yet, nor are the Republics conquered, whatever may be said to the contrary, notwithstanding.

I am watching with interest the General Election now pending. Truly, much depends upon the new Parliament. The world-wide magnitude of the Chinese Question (1900) does not portend more to England than does the South African Question. Upon the ultimate arrangement of this latter (supposing you win the war) will hang the very life of your empire within the next half century. It is a time at which you and other enlightened Englishmen will require to act with great wisdom. I am not indulging in any vapid boasting, or party bluff. Merely as a man of education, one who knows Englishmen and England with her past traditions and history past and present, a Boer of Boers who knows his people thoroughly, I forecast out of the present situation two alternatives for the British Empire. In the one case Britain may build up for herself a lasting strength by allying to herself, through friendship, a people who are most certainly destined to be as mighty a factor in the White Man's civilization as even is the United States of America. On the other hand it lies in Britain's power to range over against her, by an oppressive policy, this same important element. Should this last be the result of the forthcoming measures it will undoubtedly bear bitter fruit for Britain in the Armageddon for the world's supremacy, to which she is now undoubtedly approaching.

Time was when I used to think it would take us a century before we could step into line as a real and appreciative factor in the world's active forces; and I often feared that we, the Afrikander, would *not* be the dominant note in our constitution; but what I have seen and experienced in the last twelve months has induced me to reduce my calculation by fifty years, and to forecast as the dominant element of the future the Afrikander—not exactly as he is at present, somewhat varied perhaps, but still the Afrikander.

"Strange words, these," you may say, "at such a time, from such a place, and from such a one! The mad sayings of the imprisoned subject of an over-presumptuous, but now smashed up, little, petty Republic!"

Truly spoken, David, if you take into consideration just so much as strikes the eye in the passing moment. But I am standing on a far wider basis. I am dealing with elements I *know*, and with vast potentialities which are *proved*, as they will operate in conjunction with conditions which will inevitably ensue, as the result of contemporary events and read in the light of the past. I am now in a way speaking the passions which actuate us in the present, though in the future they will be a potent factor and not to be disregarded in determining the happiness or misfortune of your country and mine respectively.

It is for these reasons that I relegate into the hands of your now-to-be-elected (1900) legislators the good fortune or evil, in the highest degree, of England. As for ours, it is assured. Nothing can prevent it. We may pass under a cloud and the yoke of bondage for a time. But you and I may both live to see us emerge from it in the fulness of youthful strength. If England has not by then made us her friend she will have us for her enemy, and a dangerous enemy at that.

My personal adventures are too numerous to record here. I have written to my sister Nancy a few of my adventures, and she will let you read the letter if it is of interest to you.

During my eight months of active service I was two months on duty at head-quarters as one of the subordinate commandants over a district on the goldfields. Tiring of the monotony of the work I went to the front on December 17th as a private burgher in the Army of the West at Magersfontein. Subsequently I took part in the expedition which crossed the Orange River into the Western Province of the Cape Colony at Prieska.

When our little force retreated from there I was cut off while riding despatches, and had a sensational ride of nearly a thousand miles to escape capture before I got back to my commando. After that I served along the Vaal River in the capacities of Veldcornet and Commandant respectively. I was in the last stand round Johannesburg and also took part in the fighting before Pretoria, where, as already stated, I broke my ankle and was taken prisoner.

I was never hit by the enemy, though frequently under cannon and rifle fire. On the last day of fighting I was thrice struck by the splinters of shell, and only saved by the friendly interposition of a big lump of ironstone from being converted into fragments, though the concussion very nearly did for me all that was required.

At the end of it all I am quite well, but very sorry not to be still afield. I hope you and yours are well. I shall be glad to hear from you. My address is " Veldcornet F. R. Mostyn Cleaver, Transvaal Prisoner of War, Dyatalawa, Ceylon."

With very kindest wishes to yourself and Mrs. Oliver, believe me, my dear David,
  Most sincerely yours,
    (Sgd.) F. R. MOSTYN CLEAVER.

His last letter reached me fourteen days after the sad news of his death—just a year after the beginning of the war.

> Dyatalawa Camp, Ceylon,
> Oct. 14th, 1900.

My dear Mother,

The last mail brought to hand your letter of Aug. 26th, addressed to Cape Town.

You rightly surmise that I can receive your letters, and so could you mine, if only they were less severely censored by our brave General de Wet.

I am surprised the authorities in Cape Town, to whom you have so frequently applied for news of me, do not write to tell you where I am. They forwarded to me one of your letters to themselves, with the injunction that I was to write to you. Needless to say I have done so frequently.

It is very good of Major McPherson to take so much trouble to find Robin. Robin is one of my most cherished associations, and his recovery would afford me the greatest gratification.

How's Jim? If he were here he could have lots of jackals and mierkats. There are plenty of them here and very tame. They come into our huts sometimes at night to pick up scraps. About three o'clock one morning, some time back, one of the Motherlanders Ambulance doctors came to wake me, saying: "Sta op! de jachkals is wier hier. De buiten deur heb ik gesloten, en kunnen wy hem mooi in de hoek vastkeeren." I in turn woke up a landdrost and an engineer. We all armed ourselves with knives and hammers and axes, and guided by the sound of gnawing and scratching, advanced in a gradually narrowing circle towards a heap of baskets, piled up in one corner. After considerable manœuvring and guarded pokes into the surrounding darkness we hedged in a healthy looking rat, who dodged all our efforts to slay him. We all went back to bed looking sheepish. Our hunting parties are come to an end. The jackal courses through the hut unmolested, whilst we go through life contemptuously branded by our companions with the names of Kitchener, Methuen, and others, who of late have had similar futile experiences in the art of "surrounding."

Your letters are a very great pleasure to me; but do not harrow yourself by picturing me as the downcast exile wilting under the stress of confinement. If you do so your picture is entirely erroneous. I am serenely happy. The only tincture of unhappiness—and this is really and truly very great—is derived from the fact that I am debarred from further participation

Off to Ceylon

in the great struggle of my country. Except for this I am, as stated, serenely happy. The British Government supplies us with food sufficient to live healthily upon, and in addition gives us recreations and a hut to live in. I brought plenty of clothes with me, and if they wear out I shall wear rags with a keener gratification—knowing it is for my country's cause —than ever I derived from the best broadcloth in the past. All those incidents of daily life, ranking under the name of inconveniences, afford me a profound pleasure. A period of "hard" in the cells at Kandy, on a point of principle, would afford me an exquisite delight. I am firmly and serenely convinced of the great and dominant future of the Boer. In the first place I do not for a moment believe he will lose this war; and in the second place, *supposing* he should do so, his humiliation will only be a temporary, transient, and quickening incident in the life of the nation. I shall once more in my lifetime walk the soil of my own free country under the shadow of the Vyfkleur, waving glorious in the sight of all the world, blotting out the record of the present troublous times! Is *that* a prospect to produce sadness?

You wish me a bright future. *There it is.* Though it is probably not the one you were thinking of. It would be under different auspices *you* would call a future bright. On this point, however, we can never be agreed. You are

English, while I am with my native Africa to the last throb of my life!

Some of my old friends, you say, are very sorry for the part I have taken and cannot explain my action. From the bottom of my heart I pity them; for it shows they are incapable of appreciating singlehearted devotion to principle. Any weakling can throw in his lot with the side whose victory is likely to be almost a foregone conclusion. But to stick up for one's convictions when defeat is almost as certainly foregone, and self-interest lies all the other way, requires a *Man!*

I do not tell you these things in my letters for you to keep them to yourself. I wish you to tell them to the persons to whom they are addressed. I wish these men to know that I am glad of what I have done for my country, and only sorry my course of action was cut short by the misfortune of my capture. I wish them to understand that my patriotism is not of the kind which can flourish only so long as my country could continue to pay me a thousand a year. Even as at times I fearlessly criticized its actions when it was in the heyday of fortune, I am now able and determined to stand by it, even in this its day of extremest trouble, when the victor has proclaimed it out of existence. God forget me the day I forget my native land in its extremity!

It appears to me an utter futility to write you letters, for you never receive them. But I write in the hope that one or other of them may reach you and afford you some consolation.

I am sending this to the care of old Mr. Mundt of the Rand Club. I have not yet heard anything of the girls, though that is chiefly owing to myself. My letter to them was so long and took so much time to get finished that it went to post only a fortnight ago. It will be another three weeks ere I get a reply.

I am very, very sorry for you, my dearest Mother, that your old age is cast in such troublous times. I sincerely hope your strength will enable you to hold out against the privations of the practical siege you are undergoing now in Johannesburg. Do not allow yourself to be in any way troubled about me. I am perfectly well in all physical respects; and the certain conviction that we are going to win this war renders me mentally quite happy.

If you have not already sent me that ten pounds I asked you for some time ago, you can do so when and if convenient.

With very best love, believe me, my dearest Mother,

Ever your affectionate son,
F. R. MOSTYN CLEAVER.

But the girls, his sisters, never had his letter in his lifetime. It was detained by the Censor. After his death the authorities sent it to them.

The remittance had been somewhat delayed

because we had to get special permission at that time to send money out of the colony. But before he went into hospital he had received from me a draft for four times the amount he asked.

CHAPTER VII
THE LAST COMMANDO

N the 27th of November 1900 I made my Kafir boy drive myself and my sister to the General Post Office. It was some time since I had had a letter from Ceylon, and I went to see if there might not be one for me. There was no delivery in those days. The public had to go personally, or send a note by a messenger to enquire for letters. There was usually a crowd of anxious ones before the counter, and each was attended to alphabetically. Often one had to wait more than an hour before his turn came.

On this special morning I was in the best of spirits, chatting with one and another of the waiting crowd, until my chance came to say to the worried clerk, "Any letters for Cleaver?"

One was handed to me which, womanlike, I examined for marks of recognition. It bore the Bloemfontein postmark and the handwriting seemed familiar; but still I could not recollect whose it was. So, contrary to my usual practice of waiting until I got home to read my letters, curiosity made me open it at once. My eyes fell upon the words "The death of your son Reginald." That was all I saw. I fell upon the floor and knew little more until at a door, at which the trap stood still, I heard the sympathetic voice of Mr. Darragh say, "So the blow has fallen!"

At his house I remained some days most carefully tended by Miss Lloyd and himself. Nor were other friends behindhand in sympathetic attentions. But enough of myself.

The letter was from Dr. Brill, head of the Grey College, and enclosed a cable from Sir Charles Ridgway.

Governor, Colombo.   Bishop Bloemfontein,
                                     18th Nov. 1900.

Deeply regret F. R. M. Cleaver died to-day. Inform relatives.

In the fatal letter dated the 21st Nov. containing the terrible tidings of his death, was written:

My dear Mrs. Cleaver,

So this terrible war has claimed another victim! A young man in the bloom of life, who, by his character and talents, had such a promising future before him. He was one of my most beloved pupils, whose career I followed with great interest, and whose premature death causes me the greatest grief in the midst of all the sorrows and anxiety inseparable from the times in which we live.

J. B. BRILL.

A few days later came a letter from Bishop Webb and many another friend.

Fourteen days after this dark shadow fell, a letter was brought me through Mr. Mentz of the Rand Club. It had been written by him before the fever struck him down. A voice speaking from the grave!

I think it would be ungrateful of me to omit an acknowledgement of the great kindness shown me, for his sake, by the military against whom he had fought.

The poorer and humbler classes did not forget me either. It was a matter of daily occurrence for persons of both nationalities to come and thank me for kindnesses and services rendered them by my son whilst he was doing duty in the town in the early stages of the war.

In the Government Gazette of Johannesburg on the 28th Nov. 1900, appeared the following:

The Late Mr. Cleaver.

Deep regret will be felt at the death reported in yesterday's "Gazette" of Mr. Reginald Mostyn Cleaver, who died at Ceylon on the 18th of November of meningitis and enteric fever.

Advocate Cleaver was born in the Bethlehem district of the Orange Free State. He was educated first at St. Andrew's in Bloemfontein, then privately by his mother, and finally entered the Grey College. From there he went to England and joined the Middle Temple, where he gained several scholarships, and was called to the Bar in 1892. Returning to South Africa he, in 1897, entered the Government service of the late Z. A. Republiek, with the determination, as he expressed it, of "cleansing the Augean Stables." He was appointed second State Prosecutor of Johannesburg, and distinguished himself by unflinching energy and a rare integrity of character. These qualities soon won him the regard and admiration of all parties, and made him a universal favourite. At the outbreak of war he was appointed Veldcornet of Jeppestown, and as such went to the front and took a prominent part in the Prieska Expedition which, as everyone knows, was quickly put a stop to by Lord Kitchener's approach. On the 5th June he was taken prisoner in the fight near Pretoria, and a short time afterwards sent to Ceylon. Though of Herculean stature, he was, unfortunately, prone to weak health and fever, which now has caused untimely death. Great sympathy will be felt with his widowed mother, who is by his death bereft of the last of her sons and the only support of her old age.

Another writes on 1st December:

... the death of our dear friend, Mr. Advocate Mostyn Cleaver. Many, many in the camp will be sorry that this grand man and true friend has passed away.

Being in hospital myself since the 13th Nov.

I, on the 30th, asked an officer to ask Mr. Cleaver to come and see me. He replied Mr. Cleaver died twelve days ago. I was struck dumb with horror and grief.

A young man told me our friend was taken to hospital on the 9th and succumbed to enteric on the 18th Nov. The funeral was a very large and impressive one. A whole company of soldiers did him the last honour of shooting three salutes over his grave.

May he rest in Peace!

R. BERNSTEIN.

Church House,
Salisbury, Rhodesia,
26th Nov. 1900.

My dear friend,

I must send you a word of deepest sympathy in the terrible news from Colombo. I was just writing to Reggie when the telegram in the paper stopped me with its abrupt suddenness.

To think of those three boys and their father taken and you and I left.

May peace be on them more and more, and some of it—yea, all of it—be reflected in our lives.

Onwards and upwards, with no time for halting or regrets—that is the soldier's motto, "With the Cross (and the Crown too) of Jesus going on before."

Yours affectionately in Him,
W. GAUL
(Bp. Mashonaland).

A young friend, writing on Dec. 5th, 1900, from Dyatalawa, says:

He was the first to welcome me when I arrived here as a captive. In his hut he was elected captain. At important meetings, where matters regarding the health of the prisoners were discussed, he was elected President. He was the first to propose plans for having the youngsters in camp educated instead of letting them loaf about and waste their time in idleness. He was the one to take a lead in everything that was good. His deeds tell that he loved the good, the holy, the true, and the just. He has proved that he was willing to risk even his life and freedom for the country he loved. At Scholtznek he proved what steel he was made of—and then at Prieska.

On Sunday, Nov. 18th, 1900, our dearly beloved Reggie breathed his last. On Monday at 9 a.m. we carried his remains to their last resting place. The Reverends G. Murray, Oudtshoorn, Postma, Pretoria, and Roux, Senekal conducted the service. The large multitude attending listened in great silence that witnessed to the many broken hearts. We miss him, oh we miss him! We could not do without him! and yet we must. What the South African Republic and the Orange Free State, and even all South Africa lose in him, I leave to another, who really knows what Reggie has done in his short life, to tell.

My late father (Hoofd Commandant Ferreira) regarded him as a son. He looked upon us as brothers.

CORNELIUS FERREIRA.

Church House,
Bulawayo,
29th Sept., 1900.

My dear Reg,

I heard from your Mother that you had been sent to Colombo, so I am enclosing a note to the Bishop of Colombo to tell you I am thinking of you continually, and hoping that all will come right eventually.

* * * * * *

Write to me here and let me know if I can be of service to you.

I am, dear Reg,
Very affectionately,
(Sgd.) W. GAUL (Bp. Mashonaland).

In the book of J. M. Brink upon the captivity in Ceylon is the following:

(Translated from the Dutch)

Amongst the many lamented deaths which took place in the camp, we above all regretted the decease of Advocate Cleaver. He succumbed to fever on the 18th November, 1900. In every respect he was an enthusiastic leader of his people! In word and deed he was at all times ready to carry the needs of the prisoners of war on his heart. As brave and beloved chairman of the hut captains he ever did his best to bring the griefs of the prisoners of war to the notice of the authorities, and by this means to endeavour to soften the pain of the people. His death plunged us in sorrow, and when his remains, covered with the Vierkleur, were placed in the earth, we exclaimed "Africa has again laid a precious sacrifice on the Altar of Freedom."

The Bishop of Colombo wrote:

Colombo, Ceylon,
Feb. 26th, 1901.

My dear Mrs. Cleaver,

What I heard most of was his earnest and repeated expressions of love for his mother, and desire to keep bad news from you during his last illness.

But all agreed that in his delirium his thoughts were continually of the war, and of plans connected with it. He hoped, they told me, to get parole and go to India. (N.B.—This he had just received before he entered the hospital.—Ed.)

Sister Lucy (almost at the last) had been pressing him to take some milk, and he had been refusing, saying it was useless. After a while he said very tenderly: "I will take it for the Lord's sake—for the dear Lord's sake." I gather that he said this to please her, for he was very grateful for all that was done for him. These were his last words.

The cemetery of the Boer prisoners of war adjoins that which I consecrated for the British. The graves in it are arranged in perfect order, and each is marked with a very handsome cross made of very fine wood supplied by the Government. It will be some satisfaction to you that your son's grave is close to the consecrated ground of our own Church, and the Psalm and hymn "Jesus lives" were sung by the soldiers close beside it.

Mrs. Copleston has probably told you or your daughters how great was the shock and disappointment when we heard of your son's death, just as she started for our house in the hills, where she hoped he was to visit her, on a special parole offered by the Governor for the purpose.
      R. I. COLOMBO.

        J'burg.,
        15—1—01.

Dear Mrs. Cleaver,

I had hoped to have seen you before this and expressed my deep sympathy with you in your great grief. I was greatly shocked to read the sad news as I knew how terribly you would feel the loss of your son. Everyone I have met who knew Mr. Cleaver seemed so sorry at his loss and spoke in such high terms of him, both as an official and as a private individual.

In all sympathy,
   Yours sincerely,
     LIONEL BANON (Major).

Ravenswood,
Bloemfontein,
Nov. 26, 1900.

My dear Mrs. Cleaver,

You have already received the sad message which I was commissioned by the Government to convey to you.

. . . I am indeed grieved and distressed that the occasion of my writing to you, after so many years have passed since our frequent meetings and common share in the life and work of the Church, should be only to offer you but a poor expression of deepest sympathy with you in such a heavy sorrow and trial. . . .

ALLAN WEBB (Bishop).

Coronado, U.S.A.,
Jan. 9th, 1901.

Dear Sister Margy,

I see no reason for the convention of black bordered paper in what our utterly wise Father has done for our Reg. in taking him out of the harsh school of probation just when his heart and mind were transfused by a fierce and self-sacrificing love of a high ideal. I am sorry for myself; I am sorry for you; yet I can see and admit that it is grand, it is palpable proof of our Reg.'s high spiritual state for his Father to have removed him from probation to a fixed state of eternal usefulness at a moment when his heart was full of an unselfish devotion to some of the best and highest and purest ideals which ever animate the human mind.

For our Reg.—his warfare is accomplished.

YOUR OTHER REG.

> The Camp,
> Dyatalawa,
> 15th Feb., 1901.

Dear Mrs. Cleaver,

Poor Reginald joined me on the " Mohawk " S.S. at Cape Town about the 19th of July. We shared the same cabin from there to Colombo. When we arrived here on the 9th August we were also in the same hut, No. 27. He was never out of camp without me and was looking well and in the best of spirits. He was beloved by all. He was our hut captain and the leader of all sports amongst his fellow prisoners of war. He was always speaking of going on tour through India, if he could get parole, until the war should be settled in South Africa. Shortly before he got sick he received a draft from you and he told me of it. He said: " The poor old Mother has sent me too much, but I will not touch a cent of it, but try and make my trip to India with it." The first day I noticed him to be seedy was on 5th Nov. On the 6th he was still very hot and feverish. The doctor came, and on the 8th he was still the same. On the 9th the doctor ordered him to hospital. I helped to carry him on a mattress. His hat was over his face. At the door of the hospital a young Ladybrander, a former schoolmate, lifted the hat and cried in alarm "Oh! it's Reggie." This man was one of the hospital helpers, a very kind-hearted fellow, and attended to Reginald part of the time of his illness. He seemed to get on very well until the 18th, when he got suddenly worse. I visited him for the second time that day about four o'clock, as I was afraid he was growing worse. When I arrived at his bedside I saw my poor Reginald was slowly and surely dying. He held out his two hands to me and gripped me, oh, so fast, and shouted so loud to me, "Come here! is that ship ready to sail for India?" He got so excited that the nurse told me it was not advisable for me to remain in his sight. I cannot describe to you how I felt. I waited about, knowing he was near the end. He died at a quarter to five.

My poor friend was buried on the 19th Nov. 1900 with military honours and under the Transvaal flag—the only man to whom this honour has been granted.

A cross is being carved by Commandant Brale, a German who knew your son in London. The inscription is F. R. Mostyn Cleaver, Johannesburg, died 18th Nov. 1900, aged 29. Psalm 114, v. 7 (which reads: "Turn again then to thy rest, O my soul, for the Lord hath had mercy on thee").

I do feel for you, knowing how you have been against this war. Dear Mrs. Cleaver, we all see now, when it is too late, our eyes are opened.

Dear "Dick," as he was called in our camp, was beloved by all without one exception. He was the leader and captain of all our clubs and sports. We used to do our own washing together out at the waterfall and were happy in doing so, singing together like schoolboys. He often spoke of you as a loving Mother and of how you used to worry about him. He never looked downhearted, but was always full of fun. God rest his soul!

From yours respectfully,
THOS. M. MENTON.

Dyatalawa,
5 Feb., 1901.

Dear Mrs. Cleaver,

I can assure you that your dear departed son was held in high esteem throughout the whole camp. He had a warm heart for his people, and up to the time of his illness he was always engaged in the cause of the burghers here, to promote their welfare in the peculiar circumstances in which we are situated.

His funeral was very impressive. A proper officer's funeral was granted him. A great number of people were allowed to attend, and there was a general expression of sorrow in the camp. I performed the funeral service, and General the Rev. Roux also gave testimony to all his good acts for the burghers and for our fatherland in the past.

REV. P. POSTMA.

Special Ward,
Boer Hospital,
Dyatalawa,
Jan. 15, 1901.

Dear Lady,

I thought, as your son passed away in this ward, you might like to hear from me. We did all we could for him. I myself tended him and my nurses also did all they could, and the doctors were most attentive and grieved over his death. He would, at the end, only take his food from me. On the last occasion I said " Do try and take this milk!" He looked up, and after a long look, he said: "I will, because of the good God," and then he seemed to mistake me for someone else, and added, " I will for old friendship's sake." He spoke very little more and was not properly conscious.

The funeral was a very large one and had all military honours. Of course I went. The cemetery is close by on the lonely mountain side. Mr. Postma took the service. The grave is marked by a simple wooden cross. God comfort you, dear lady, as one whom his mother comforteth.

SISTER LUCY.

INDEX

Page numbers in bold refer to the introduction, in letters to the preface and in roman to the main text.

Banon, Major Lionel, 109, 195
Begbie, William, 102, 107–8, 120, 164
Bernstein, R., 173, 191
Blackburn, Douglas, **20**
Boshoff, Hans, 11, 136
Botha, Gen. Louis, 118, 134, 137, 170
Brall, Fritz, x
Bramley, Charlie, 173
Brand, J. H., **10**
Brill, Dr Johannes, **15**, ix, 188
Brink, Jan, **16**, **32**, 193
Brink, Richard, 116, 124–5, 173
Brohier, R. L., **36**, **39**
Carey-Hobson, Mary Ann, **7**
Chamberlain, Joseph, 30, 101

Index

Cleaver, Anne Fenton, **13**, **19**, 128
Cleaver, Joseph Mostyn, **8**, **12**, **15**
Cleaver, Letitia, **13**, 128
Coleman, Walter, 46, 74, 136
Cronje, Gen. Piet, **12**, 62, 66, 77, 85, 90
Darragh, Mr, 105, 107, 124–5, 135, 164, 188
de la Rey, Gen. J. H., 128, 136
de Villiers, Jaap, **11**, xi, 136
de Wet, Gen. C. R., **16**, 110, 113, 118, 122, 136, 170, 172, 181
Engelbrecht, H. E., **34**
Esser, Mr Justice, 4, 36
Fenton, Myfanwy Mary, **13**, **21**
Fenton, Reginald, **7–9**, **12**, **21**, 162, 197
Ferreira, Cornelis, **16**, 38, 42, 159, 172, 193
Ferreira, Gen. Ignatius, **16**, 6, 16, 36–8, 40–4, 48–51, 63, 65, 77, 79, 86, 166, 193
Gaul, Bishop, 108, 191, 193
Hastings, Beatrice, **1**
Hertzog, Gen. J. B. M., xi
Holloway, Jim, **27**
Jacobsz, Louis, 19, 45, 78
Jooste, Commandant Koos, **22**, 92
Joubert, Gen. Piet, **7**
Judilwitz, Hermann, 93
Kingsley, Mary, **35**
Kitchener, Lord, 61–62, 94, 143, 145, 166, 182, 190
Kock, Gen., **33**, 16

Index

Kruger, Paul, 29, 102, 170
Leipoldt, C. Louis, **19**
Lewis, J. P., **36**
Liebenberg, Gen. Piet, 74, 85–7, 90–1
'Lucy, Sister', **34–5**, 194, 200
Lyttelton, Rev. A. V., 108, 135
Mackenzie, Colonel, 107, 124
Macnab, Roy, **5**
Macpherson, Major, 119–20, 181
Marais, Eugène N., **17**
Menton, Tom, 44, 47, 49, 116, 123–4, 173, 199
Meyer, Rudolf, 96, 125
Milner, Alfred, 29, 62
Murray, Rev. G., 192
Nathan, Manfred, **5**, **9**, **11**, **19–20**
Nevinson, Henry, **16**
O'Flaherty, Mr, 41, 118, 124–5
Oliver, David, 173, 181
Pohl, Victor, **32**
Poore, Major, 102, 104–5, 162–3
Postma, Rev., 192, 200
Poulier, L. G., **34**
Prinsloo, Gen. Marthinus, **12**, 36, 172
Reitz, Deneys, **6**
Reitz, F. W., **17**, **19–20**, 14
Roberts, Lord, 97, 100, 102, 109, 120, 128, 136, 163, 167–8, 170
Roux, Rev., 192, 199

Index

Schoeman, Karel, **33**
Sheppard, Mr, 44, 47, 78, 161
Smith, Ethel, **22**
Smuts, J. C., **17**, **20**, xi–xii, 2, 19–20, 78
Steenkamp, Gen. L. P., 53, 74, 85–6, 88, 92
Stockenstrom, Andreas, 19, 103, 134
Styx, Mr, 79, 135, 161
Thomas (groom), 44, 100, 107, 121
van Reenen, Frikkie, 114, 136
van Reenen, Johannes, 38, 114, 136
van Rooyen, C. J., **31**, 172
Viljoen, Ben, **32**
Villebois-Mareuil, G., Comte de, 114, 136
Vincent, Colonel, 137–8
Webb, Bishop Allen, 189, 196
Wessels, Elria, **25**
Wright, Colonel, 107–9, 122, 164–5